D0863210

I CAN'T FORGET

A Journey through Nazi Germany and WWII

By Gudrun (Koppe) Everett

Library of Congress Control Number: 2006909007

ISBN: 1-4196-5070-X

Publisher: BookSurge, LLC
North Charleston, South Carolina

Manufactured in the United States of America

Composition and cover design by Christian Everett

I wish to express my profound respect and love for my late parents and my two older brothers. With humility I acknowledge the higher powers that led me with invisible hands to survive and to eventually find safety and happiness.

I dedicate these autobiographic pages to my beloved husband of 55 years and, with gratitude for his technical assistance, to my dear son, Christian.

I.
Falkenberg

1931 – 1936

Freilassing

1936 – 1939

I CAN'T FORGET

My family lived in Falkenberg on the Elster – a tributary to the Elbe River – in Saxon-Anhalt, Germany. Born in 1931, I was the youngest of three children; my two brothers, Ernst and Joachim, were five and seven years older than I. When I was born, my mother employed Elsa as a "Kindermaedchen," a nanny. She was to assist with the new baby in the household. At the time, Elsa was only in her teens and, from the very beginning, her devotion to the new baby and her trustworthiness earned her my mother's confidence.

Falkenberg. (Bez. Halle). Friedrichstraße.

My father's house, Friedrich Strasse in Falkenberg on the Elster, Sachsen Anhalt, place of my birth, August 11, 1931 (above).

1994, after the collapse of the Soviet Union and German re-unification, visitors in rental car: Zach and I (left).

Evidently these circumstances are among the reason that Elsa's image is as endearing in my memory as that of my own mother's. As unlikely as it may seem, because of Elsa I can actually remember riding in a stroller. It must have been in the fall when one evening I saw for the first time a full autumn moon in the dark sky, while Elsa pushed me in my stroller to her parents' home. The rhythmic steps of Elsa's feet were the only sound that broke the silence of the moonlit path as she pushed the stroller. Along the way, I recall having a friendly conversation with the moon while it seemed to follow us, shining down on my stroller. In fact, I recall to this day that during my conversation there were moments of uneasiness whenever the moon disappeared behind the black crowns of trees silhouetted against the sky. I rejoiced each time when its silvery disk appeared again between the openings in the tall trees – reassuring me that the moon was still shining on me and that I could resume my chatter.

It was during that evening when the understanding of "mondsuechtig" was created in my mind. While pushing the stroller, my intense conversation with the moon appeared to worry Elsa and she warned me several times not to keep looking at the moon – that it could cause some mysterious harm. Being "mondsuechtig," or moonstruck, in those days was commonly understood to lead to somnambulism. It was the root of becoming afflicted with sleepwalking. That evening, Elsa was genuinely concerned that my staring at the moon while lying in the stroller could trigger my walking in my sleep some day. Indeed, it was a few years later, when I was eight or nine, that I recall several incidents when I woke up standing at the rail on top of the stairway, or when I woke up downstairs standing in the kitchen – wondering why.

Just how much Elsa loved me as a child I came to appreciate only years later. I now recognize her total dedication by the fact that, on that moonlit evening when she pushed me in the stroller, she was actually taking me home with her – to her father and mother – and this, after taking care of me all week. Today I realized that Elsa wanted me to be with her even on Sunday, her day off.

I learned to call Elsa's parents Papa and Tante Martha. Papa had a handlebar mustache and he smoked a pipe that hung precariously from between his teeth as he moved about. He was a retired railroad conductor, and often he wore the dark blue jacket of his railroad uniform with shiny gold buttons. Tante Martha's hair was neatly pulled back straight into a bun at the nape of her neck, and she usually had a large apron tied around her waist. Because she baked huge sheet-cakes covered with plums or streusels, their house always smelled wonderfully of yeast dough.

Outside in the tidy yard, there was a doghouse where Papa's big dog was tied up. It was the highlight of my visit when Papa put a harness on the big dog, hitched him to a small wooden cart and then propped me up inside the cart to sit next to his hoe, a trowel and Tante Martha's basket that held slices of cake and a jug of cider. Papa and his big dog then pulled the cart to the asparagus field at the base of the great windmill. There in the field he worked on his knees, using his trowel as he piled the soil into mounds to cover the tender asparagus shoots. While watching Papa, the big dog sat next to me on the edge of the field under a shady hedge.

Despite my fond memories of Elsa from the beginning, there is one that remains painful to this day. I had eaten a chocolate candy that must have smeared my face. I suddenly felt a determined wipe across my mouth and, to my shock, I saw that Elsa used spit to moisten the corner of her handkerchief and get at the dried chocolate around my mouth. I recall my loud and angry protestations and that I struggled to push her hand away. Dear Elsa never found out that I CAN'T FORGET to this day her spittle on that hanky...

With Elsa by the asparagus field and windmill (left), near Elsa's house (right), 1932-33

LIFE AT KNEE LEVEL

Beginning with my earliest memories, the kitchen was the arena for our family's idiosyncrasies. It was where I ran to when I had to cry, and Elsa was there to make for me a slice of bread with molasses, and the kitchen was where Elsa fretted over my chronic constipation.

With the remedial promise of prunes, she gave me manna to eat. Manna was a strange looking thing; it looked like a smooth, brown, wooden bean pod as long as my child-size forearm. The shell was much like that of a pecan, but softer, so that one could peel it with the fingernail. The inside held cellulose-like disks; they were seeds that were coated with a dark brown, sweet-tasting substance. Many years later, I learned that what they called "manna" really was a carob bean.

Elsa always helped me get started with peeling the shell, but then she left me on my own. It was the most frustrating task to get at those sweet tasting seed-disks and then, when I did manage to free one of them, there was not much to it. I put it into my mouth and sucked a few times and the sweet substance was gone, but the disk-shaped husk was still in my mouth. I do not know why nobody worried that I might swallow that seed disk by mistake, which could have led to a much more dangerous condition than my constipation. What made my predicament of retention so complicated was that both my mother and Elsa had the fixed notion that wholesome regularity should happen by eight o'clock every morning. They extolled the magic of this biological hour above anything pertaining to the clock. To impose their hypothesis, Elsa put me on a children's commode right in the kitchen under the window "to watch you!" as she said. The commode was comfortable and low enough for me to rest my feet on the floor, and it even had a back and armrests. Every few minutes I whined: "Can I get up now?" Then somebody checked, and back down I went, a finger waggled in front of my face, and "eat your manna!" was the order.

There was no question that they were correct about my chronic condition – however, my daily confinements upon the children's commode rarely led to conclusive solutions. Instead – I believe – they made things shut down more firmly as a reaction to my knee level environment. After all, while I was down there under the window, the others above me were free to do whatever they wanted. There were loud voices when my brothers quarreled about their model plane, Elsa clattered with the breakfast dishes, Murrax – our terrier – barked with excitement as my mother prepared to take him for a morning walk – and I just sat there with the sticky manna in my hand.

In retrospect, I note that Elsa had a pattern of devices that put me repeatedly into sitting positions whenever I was in the kitchen; perhaps they were her means to keep me from underfoot and "to watch you!" – as she said. One such connivance was to push a kitchen chair against the front of the cabinet, then to pick me up and set me – my feet straight out – on the chair in front of the drawer. It was so clever when she pulled out the drawer above my legs and fitted it snuggly against my stomach to wedge me comfortably between the back of the chair and the face of the drawer.

My exhilaration was indescribable when I saw for the first time the entire content of our household junk-drawer all at once – right there before my eyes! I could not believe that I finally could reach to the back of the drawer with the full length of both arms. It meant no more stretching and groping around blindly inside the junk-drawer! I could actually reach every clothespin, bottle opener and rubber band without any strain. "Don't throw things on the floor!" Elsa warned, and for a moment she watched my feverish hands inside the drawer, and then quickly she removed a mouse-trap and some thumbtacks. "You might hurt yourself," she explained. She walked away to come back with a wooden cutting board that she placed across part of the open drawer. "Now you can put things on the board to examine them," she said.

Elsa was so clever, and I loved Elsa. Between me and Elsa, the junk drawer became a bond of silent understanding, especially on rainy days. And occasionally she would find me slumped into the drawer – fast asleep.

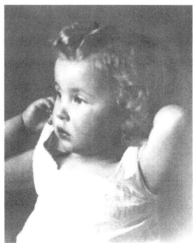

Gudrun Johanna Ingeborg Koppe, born August 11, 1931

With Ernst.

FREILASSING – NAMES AND TITLES

Freilassing was about twenty kilometers from Salzburg. In fact, the town was the official border crossing from Germany into Austria. In 1936, my father was mayor of Freilassing. At that time, when a man held a public position in Germany, his wife was addressed by her husband's title or rank – a curious custom. Hence, if a man was in charge of the railroad station, his wife was the Frau Direktor; this was the case for the museum director's wife, as well as for the orchestra conductor's. For the same reason, the police officer's wife was Frau Inspektor, the doctor's wife was Frau Doktor, and my mother was usually addressed as Frau Buergermeister...

As mayor, my father was mostly occupied with building schools and hospitals, and he planned housing and tourism, and he always had many people around him. At my age of five, I evidently fulfilled my father's inclination to pamper and to dote, which he clearly could not do with my older brothers. I must have brought out a playful side in his otherwise serious nature. For this reason, in his duties as the town's official, my role could have been viewed as his personal eccentricity, because he took me along wherever he chose. That's why I often sat in city hall near his desk in an overstuffed chair with a coloring book, a kaleidoscope, or busy cutting rows of paper dolls.

His office occupied the second floor of city hall. It was a large room with windows that overlooked the city square with its typically Bavarian Maypole. The large walnut table in his office was cluttered with blueprints of building projects, bridges and sewage systems. He spent much time talking on the phone and was known for his ability to take two calls at the same time while dictating a letter. When he received a visitor, he first pointed at me, "This is Bippi," he said. I slid off the chair to shake hands and curtsey, and then I climbed back into my chair. Sometimes visitors came prepared with a lollipop for me before getting down to business with my father; and I remember when the water commissioner offered me a cigar, after he gave one to the mayor.

In his position, my father also served as justice of peace, and he frequently performed civil weddings. Occasionally, after the ceremony he was invited to join the wedding party – that is when he took "Bippi" along. Some wedding parties were very noisy and often I dodged sweaty polka dancers at knee level. At one wedding, the dinner made me sick. I will never forget the greasy roast goose, prune-stuffed potato dumplings, strawberry punch and butter-cream torte for dessert. To recover, I was laid to bed in the mother of the bride's bedroom. Most of the time, though, we did not stay long at wedding parties.

Among the Buergermeister's diverse responsibilities was the one of giving speeches; that is when I was confined to a seat in an auditorium. It was there that I first became conscious of time, that time was a relentless force that held me suspended. I felt helpless because, where normally I knew how to deal with frustration by either crying or tugging someone's sleeve, during my father's speeches I learned to be passive and to wait. Actually, I seldom understood what he was saying. At first, I listened for familiar-sounding words, and there were a few like, "We must try..." or "It is with your help" – or something like that; but I seldom found out what he was talking about. People around me clapped whenever he paused, and I clapped too because it was fun. I knew that speeches ended when the applause lasted a little longer – the signal to the elusive end of my helpless suspension in time. I listened anxiously for the one lengthy, final applause – so we could go home.

My mother was born in Rosenheim, Bavaria, but she grew up in Munich. She passed down to me the memories of her own childhood. She had three sisters, and the youngest of her siblings was a brother, my uncle Emil. Her father had been a "Court Jeweler," a title of excellence in his trade during the time of the Bavarian Monarchy. Her mother's household was that of urban Bürgers. They lived in Munich on Theadiner Strasse, an elegant apartment section near the opera. They also owned a vacation chalet in the mountains near Garmisch Partenkirchen.

My mother took great pleasure in sewing, especially lace-edged nightgowns and personal lingerie. Perhaps her memories of impeccable grooming during her childhood made it of great importance whenever she completed for me a new set of fine muslin bloomers with a drop bottom, an attached bodice and garters. Of significance was the drop bottom – she considered it a superior feature. When her friend, Frau Dennert, came to tea, she showed her my new bloomers, also some other lacy garments she had worked on. The bloomers reached just above my knees and exposed the fine Brussels lace when I bent over. These were some measures of opulence during my early childhood and, perhaps, during my mother's childhood as well.

From the earliest time that I remember, I could sing Schubert Lieder and several opera arias, as the one of the Azocena from "La Traviata;" and I knew Mimi's "Es waechst mir die Rose am Fenster" of *La Boheme* in German, because I grew up with opera arias at ten in the morning. My mother's fine voice was part of our household, and some of her routine repertoire became a feature of my childhood. For many years, I assumed that everybody's mother sang arias. She played piano well enough to accompany herself from opera scores. When she married my father, my mother brought the Boesendorfer grand piano with her. It was the same piano she had when she was at the Royal Bavarian Opera in Munich, the "Hoftheater" in the years following the First World War and which is, today, the Bavarian State Opera. As a dramatic soprano, my mother was defined as a Wagnerian singer. In fact, I found out that my name Gudrun came from one of the characters in Richard Wagner's Nibelungen Ring, a Norse mythology in which Siegfried was the husband of Gudrun. It was a very difficult story...

My mother had several photographs of her opera career, one as Elsa in Lohengrin, and there were group pictures of her among other singers with Bruno Walter at the piano. He wore a tuxedo and the ladies wore beautiful gowns. Another picture was of my mother in costume as Lenore in "Cavalleria Rusticana," and she showed me a program where she appeared at the la Scala in 1919. Famous names among her contemporaries at the opera were woven into her reminiscences – names such as chamber singer Karl Erb, Ilse Ivogyn, the tenors Benjamino Gigli, and Leo Slezak. She told me that Leo Slezak was stout and a very funny man and, between curtain calls, he wiped his nose on the velvet sleeve of his costly costume.

Our house in Freilassing had a terrace overlooking the park. In the summer, we ate Sunday breakfast or lunch there under a sun umbrella. Often, after I had my hair shampooed, my mother, sitting in one of the wicker chairs, would comb it and tell me to stay in the sun to allow the hair to dry. For special occasions, she made long spiral curls by twisting the comb as she ran it through the length of my damp hair, shaping thick sausage-like curls that draped over my shoulders. She called this Sunday-hairdo Schiller-locken." I knew that Friedrich Schiller was a German poet – like Goethe – and from pictures of Schiller I had seen, he too wore spiral curls. In Salzburg, at the wonderful pastry shop "Cafe Mozart," one could also buy Schillerlocken, but they were flaky pastry tubes filled with whipped cream and dusted with powdered sugar. Other times my mother braided my hair into tight pigtails above my ears, and then she looped the ends back to the root of each pigtail, where she fastened them with ribbons. She called this hairdo "Affenschaukeln," (monkey-swings). She gave funny names to everything...

My mother adored the Alps. She knew many of the ski resorts. Some of them she associated with her youth when she was an avid skier. In fact, she explained that the slight irregularity of her tooth on the right side was caused by a skiing accident. It must have been terrible because she described something about a fir tree that she failed to outmaneuver on a steep slope.

Often on Sundays, we all went to one of my mothers' favorite mountains, the "Hoegel." She and Elsa packed a rucksack with extra sweaters, some hardboiled eggs, salami sandwiches and binoculars. My brothers and my father put on their lederhosen with the leather suspenders. From the outset, these deerskin shorts, a typically Bavarian apparel, mandated a frivolous attitude by any man who would wear them. It is unthinkable that a man with his knees showing and an embroidered leather flap, held in place by antler

Freilassing 1936. Ernst, Gudrun, my mother, (Hildegard Schoeninger Koppe) and Joachim.

buttons over his stomach, could be angry or ill-tempered. This is why Bavarians dance the Schuhplattler, the folkdance, when they slap their knees, or why they yodel. Of course, my father – not being a native Bavarian, but a Saxon – did not know how to yodel nor dance the Schuhplattler. Nevertheless, he wanted to look like a genuine Bavarian. In reality, because of his Saxon background and dialect, he was just like any tourists who visited the Bavarian Alps – who also liked to wear lederhosen. On these outings my mother, Elsa and I wore our dirndl dresses with the puffed sleeves, billowing skirts and iridescent taffeta half-aprons.

We needed to drive less than an hour to reach the foot of the Hoegel, a mountain with trails that gently ascended through wooded slopes and several clearings along pastures, where brown and white Simmenthal cows grazed. My mother marveled at the beautiful wild flowers among the rocks. "Look at this Enzian!" she exclaimed. It was the champagne-glass shaped flower, also known as "blue gentian," the most recognized symbol of alpine flora. In addition, there were dwarf pines, wild Erica, alpine roses and the rare and celebrated Edelweiss. She told me that these flowers must never be picked. While Elsa rested on a rock, she braided a wreath of daisies and put it on my head.

The mountain trail led to a chalet at the top of the Hoegel. With its typically shallow roof, the chalet was built of cedar logs, and flaming geraniums spilled from its window boxes. We sat on the veranda with tables and sun umbrellas, while a zither player entertained the guests. We or-

1936, Gudrun at Attasee (left), at the Hoegel (right).

dered cold lemon-soda, a thick stein of Bavarian beer for my father, soft pretzels with sweet butter, and smoked ham. The cheerful sound of the zither and the view from the veranda was the cherished reward for the three-hour hike. The surrounding panorama was of breathtaking beauty, and my mother knew the names of each mountain, among them were the Watzmann, the Gaissberg and the Stauffen.

Freilassing Gaisberg, right background.

Watzmann

Untersberg

THE KASPERL-THEATER

One of the highlights of my early childhood was the puppet theater, which in Germany is called "Kasperl-Theater," and which is named after its main character, a puppet whose appearance is that of a Jester. During my generation, a Kasperl-Theater was on most children's Christmas wish list, just as a dollhouse would be, or an erector set. Each character in the theater's cast was well known, just as Kasperl himself. There was Annerl, his love, and Seppl, a good-natured simpleton, and Gretl, who was Seppl's girl-friend. These main stars were surrounded by supporting characters, such as a policeman, the town crier, a king, a beautiful princess, a kindly grandmother, and a good fairy. Representing the evil powers were a witch, a crocodile (which symbolized a monster); and there was the terrifying devil who normally appeared on stage with lights flashing, accompanied by loud bangs and shrill whistles.

To this day, the Kasperl-Theater is a notable feature in German culture, more directly in family and community life.

Kasperl-Theaters are found at country fairs as well as school and church groups. Even in Austria, the "Europark" in Salzburg, described as the "Most beautiful Mall in Europe," features a Kasperl-Theater for the young; and during recent decades, Greek and Turkish guest workers took the German Kasperl-Theater back to their home countries.

Where did the character Kasperl come from? He is quite old. The novelist Franz Clemens Brentano, who lived between 1778 and 1842, was a major intellectual figure during the height of German Romanticism. His contemporaries were Goethe and Heine, as well as the brothers Grimm, the creators of the German treasure known as Grimm's Fairy Tales. This Brentano brought Kasperl to life in a new form of literature, a novelette, by the title "The Good Kasperl und the Beautiful Annerl," a drama of honor and idealism.

I experienced my first Kasperl-Theater on a sunny day at a folk festival, where I joined five-year-olds and others seated on benches in front of an elevated stage. Typically, the show began with the opening of the curtain to expose a colorful backdrop and occasionally mysterious lighting. As usual, Kasperl made his entrance shouting his motto: "Seid's alle da? – Habt's a Geld ah?" Which means: "Are you all here? Do you have money, too?" Thereby, having invited the audience to participate, each question evoked a raucous "Jah!!" From there on, the plot took the audience through fast-moving action. It might have begun with a scene in a mysterious forest, where Kasperl looked for his beloved Annerl. As an aside, he told the children that he needed to warn her of the monster lurking in the bushes. Immediately after he left the stage, Annerl appeared, skipping along lightheartedly and singing "Tra-la-la." Naturally, the young audience shouted to get her attention, and to tell her that Kasperl had just been looking for her to warn of the dangerous monster in the bushes. As the drama developed, more characters might join the plot. Seppl and grandmother showed up, and perhaps the Princess got kidnapped by the monster – that is when the policeman added his presence. While the action on stage became more frenetic, the audience's participation increased with loud shrieks and hoots, ever hopeful that Kasperl will bring a happy ending to the plot, when he rescued the right people from terrible injustice and looming danger.

In 1936, on Christmas Eve, I received a Kasperl-Theater of my own. I recall waiting eagerly for the tinkle of the bell, a custom that announces that the Christkindl had been behind the closed door, and that we now may enter the living room for the "Bescherung" – the opening of gifts. I can never quite describe the thrill when I found standing next to the festive tree with its glow of real candles, a genuine Kasperl-Theater. Its size was large enough for two people to stand inside and operate the puppets. Its curtain was open to reveal the stage backdrop of a street scene. Ernst explained that one could buy scripts for puppet dramas, and that he planned to add lighting to the stage. Joachim showed me a variety of interchangeable backdrops that he had painted. One was a dark forest enhanced by three-dimensional trees, and another depicted the interior of a cottage.

I spent most of Christmas Eve behind the eye-level stage to explore the clever features needed to play Kasperl-Theater. Joachim had also very thoughtfully placed hooks along the inside from which several puppets were hung, enabling nimble hands to rapidly slip inside and make the puppets appear on stage in quick order. I closely examined the main character, Kasperl, my hero, recognizable by his pointed jester-cap with the small bell at its tip. Then I slipped my hand inside the terrible devil with his fierce face and black horns. I swept him in soaring motions through the space of the stage. To stress the horror of his presence I hissed and howled in a high-pitched voice – when I, myself, suddenly became frightened. I hastily hung the devil back on his hook and stepped out from behind the stage to join the safety of my family under the beautiful Christmas tree. To calm my soul, I climbed on my mother's lap and ate a big almond Lebkuchen…

"DERRE" IS MY NAME

L ooking from our balcony through the trees of the park, one could see the yellow facade of the stately villa. In the small Bavarian town of Freilassing, it was known as the "Wrede Villa," named after the owner of the large sawmill and parquet-floor manufacturer. The first time I rode my scooter near its front steps I noticed that the entrance was boarded up and that most of the windows were shuttered. I had never seen an empty house before, and I stood on the path and studied its mystery. I was awed by its silence.

Sometime later, just as I was going to walk over to the villa again, I heard my mother's anxious voice from the terrace call me back. She explained that I must never ever go near the "Wrede Villa," because there may be holes that I could fall into, or entire staircases could fall on top of me. That is when I decided not to tell her that I had already seen Ernst and Joachim crawl out of the coal chute by the side of the service entrance to the villa a few days ago. Again, here was an example when they did things long before I even thought of doing them. Actually, my brothers, being five and seven years older than I, consistently were ahead of me. From the time I was four years old, I often felt that they did not want me around because I was a nuisance to them – and the other reason was that I had gotten them into trouble several times when I told my parents about their secrets. Knowing their secrets gave me a dizzying sense of power, an equalizing tool whenever I chose to tattle. That's what happened when they used my mother's best hairbrush to tar the canvas of the kayak they had built, or when Ernst with his airplane jumped off the second floor balcony using – without asking permission – my mother's wicker chair, to which he had mounted wings made of espalier slats that held stretched pairs of her brocade sheets. What was extra painful to me was their complaint that I should get at least half of the spankings they had gotten.

Contrary to these difficult dynamics between my big brothers and me, there were occasions when Ernst, the younger of the two, appeared definitely endearing. Those were the rare moments when he called me by the nickname he had invented for me, which was "Derre." He used it only when he inadvertently expressed affection for me, or when he assumed the condescending role of a big brother. To translate "Derre" into English is no easy task, it is an exercise for the Thesaurus, but worth the effort, because it reveals that "Derre" in the Saxon dialect stands for something that is small, thin, insignificant, runt-like, and dried up. It was always touching when he called me "Derre."

So it was on a Sunday afternoon, when Elsa had gone to the movies and my parents drove away in their Opel to visit friends, leaving Ernst and Joachim in charge of their five year old sister. It was not long before they decided to go to the gazebo that was located in the park between the villa and the mayor's house. Again, I had the feeling that my having to tag along was a nuisance to them. I sat down on a big rock in front of the gazebo, when Joachim suddenly reached into the pocket of his leather pants and pulled out a pack of "66" brand cigarettes – right there before my eyes! Out of nowhere, Ernst had matches in his hands to light Joachim's cigarette and then his own. My mouth dropped open. I was speechless. I could not believe this! They both were smoking cigarettes in front of me! I sure will tell mother about this secret as soon as she comes home. Then Ernst, leaning down in his endearing way, said: "Derre, want to take a puff of my cigarette?" while holding it near my lips. This was getting to be simply amazing – now they are even making me a partner to their secrets! "Go ahead, Derre," Ernst said in this rare moment of affection, "one puff won't matter." This time he put the cigarette against my lips and I quickly sucked a mouthful of smoke. Gee, I now was even a participant in their secrets!

After they finished their cigarettes, they started to walk toward the coal chute at the villa. "Derre, want to go inside the villa?" asked Ernst. "I'll go in first and then catch you when you follow." With that, he disappeared into the opening. Joachim, grabbing my hands, said "Hang on! There's a crate inside the cellar at the base of the chute, and Ernst will catch you." With that, he lowered me into the chute where Ernst helped me gently to the ground. Joachim followed directly. With disbelief, I realized that I again was in the middle of their secrets. Then they took my hands and led me from the dark cellar up the stairs. After walking through a pantry and a kitchen, we entered a huge hall with an extraordinary parquet floor, intricate designs of exotic woods of all colors. The rooms had enormous fireplaces, and I had never before heard my own voice as I did inside these large halls. I made beautiful echoes as we walked through the empty Wrede Villa.

Later, just before dinner, Joachim silently put his finger against his lips, a signal to remind me not to tell anyone about our secrets, while Ernst, sitting down next to me at the table, whispered in my ear, "You must never again tattle, Derre – or else we'll tell Mother that you smoke cigarettes..."

"Derre" with Ernst and Joachim, 1938 (left).
My parents with pet deer, lamb and turkey in Freilassing, 1938 (right).

HAUSMUSIK

Both my parents were musicians. It took me years to figure out what happened on those occasions when they made music. Traditionally in Germany, such moments were called "Hausmusik" – which was an admirable endeavor for a family on a Sunday afternoon – but then I have not yet told the story.

It is necessary to first explain that my father was a military musician during WWI. At that time to meet the criterion as a member of the Kaiser's Heavy Cavalry marching and parade band, he had to play a number of instruments. These high standards were the reason that my father played seven instruments – each one characteristic of splendid German march music. They included brass instruments such as the cornet and the trumpet as well as most reed instruments. There was one instrument, however, that my father played for his own enjoyment – which was not suitable for the Kaiser's cavalry parades – it was the violin. Except when used by a concert virtuoso, or in chamber music ensembles, the use of the violin in Germany suggested a "Stehgeiger," which is a diminished rank among violinists. To be a Stehgeiger means to be a violinist who stands up all night as a member of some small salon ensemble in the corner of an elegant tearoom in a fine hotel – which, of course, my father was not part to. Nevertheless, he did play the violin, and very well. The violin seemed to give him the opportunity to make music with emotion – something Germans call "Schmaltz" – and, of course, none of my father's military instruments allowed for emotional liberties. Brass and march music was played within a rigid frame of "one-two-three-four" – strict and without the slightest divergence from a metric beat – "or else soldiers would fall over, and the horses would stumble!" That is how he explained the importance of keeping proper time. Still, I loved his playing a certain Scherzo by Fritz Kreisler, quite the opposite of military march music. It was a piece for the violin that called for a distinct flair and showmanship, even weaving from the waist – not at all like music for marching or when leading a parade on horseback. When my father played Kreisler's Scherzo, it brought out his true love for the violin. The composition contained accelerations and ritardandos and it showed off those rare falsetto notes, high and ephemeral, that imitate the song of a canary. In fact, the title of the Scherzo was "Canary." It was a character piece that my father played with great bravura.

I need to explain my mother's musical background as well. In comparison to my father's, her genre was at the extreme opposite end of the musical spectrum. My mother had been an opera singer and, being capable to accompany herself when necessary, she also was a good pianist. What mattered was that as a singer, her music was deeply emotional – it was drama, glorious suffering and sublime pathos. For these reasons, her music was supported by a vague meter of timing, merely enough to support the beginning and the ending phrases of her arias, whereas my father's stern "one-two-three-four" count would have caused my mother's Michaela to die prematurely, and her Elsa in Lohengrin would have frozen into a state of tetanus during the first act.

It was another Sunday afternoon that I can't forget, when they went into the music room – with the best of intentions – to make "Hausmusik." The plan was that my mother was to accompany on the piano my father's violin playing. Behind the closed door, I could hear my mother strike the "middle-G" on her Boesendorf grand for my father to tune his violin. Then there were hasty comments on what they wanted to play. After some shuffling with pages, I could hear my father's tapping toe and a "one-two-three-four," instructing my mother about the tempo he had in mind. She then followed his suggestion as her hands played the keys to accompany my father's violin. It sounded beautiful, but suddenly my mother's playing began to lag behind slightly, only to speed up again, as if trying to compensate for the delay. In my mother's style of music-making, this kind of expression is commonly known as "rubato." It was not in my father's style, however, because his violin stopped suddenly. Gathering himself, he patiently counted once more "One-two-three-four," and the music started up again. How delightful my parents' music sounded! As I listened, I knew this was perfect Hausmusik.

To my dismay, however, after a few more minutes the music stopped once again. Immediately, I heard some terse and hissing back and forth – and, once more, my father suggested with emphasis and strained intent that there should be a clear "one-two-three-four." Following his instructions, this time my mother's piano playing was loud and marchy, with strong rhythmic accentuation on the downbeat. It did not sound like her style of music at all. For a while, their playing appeared to stay on the same beat when, somehow, my mother must have felt that there was an appropriate place for a tiny riterdando. Again, my father's violin fell silent, followed by a leaden pause. Just as my father began to count again, I heard my mother's angry voice, then some sobbing and a bang produced by the abrupt slamming of the piano lid. The door flew open and my mother stormed out of the room. Through the open door, I saw my father with his violin and bow standing there alone in gloomy resignation. It was just another Sunday afternoon of what they called "Hausmusik."

THE VIEW FROM A WINDOW

Our kitchen in Freilassing was the site that left me with a jumble of childhood memories. In the rear of the house was our living room, a terrace and a park, where my father kept several deer in an enclosure with a small chalet style shelter for them. The kitchen faced the road and, from its window, I became familiar with the alpine panorama that surrounds Salzburg, Austria, which was only twenty-five kilometers from Freilassing. The massive mountains included the Stauffen and Untersberg. Dominating the center of the view from the window was the Gaisberg, its dome-shaped top in contrast to the others.

Despite my familiarity with the panorama from the age of five, the mountains continued to stir my imagination by the mystery of their dark silhouettes against the sky on clear nights. On June twenty-fourth of every year, a medieval tradition brought alpine climbers to the Gaisberg, the "Goat Mountain," to light fires on its steep slopes in celebration of "Johannis Nacht," Midsummer Night.

One late fall evening, Ernst excitedly called us to the window from where he had noticed an orange light against the dark sky on the top of the Gaisberg. After my father made a telephone call, he confirmed that the landmark hotel on the mountain was, indeed, on fire. I remember staring into the night with the windowsill under my chin, as I watched the distant glow gradually fade away. That night I learned that nobody could stop a fire on top of an alpine mountain.

Because our house was on a hill, I could see from the kitchen window a narrow pedestrian bridge that crossed several railroad tracks in the distance and, when I craned my neck to the right, I recognized through the trees a set of tracks in front of a loading ramp. The kitchen window became my periscope to events I did not yet understand. I soon observed large divisions of alpine troops, their mules and military vehicles being loaded from the ramp onto train cars.

Weeks before Hitler marched into Austria, I recall the distant rumble of cannons when the Wehrmacht conducted maneuvers at the foot of the Stauffen. The year was 1938 and, on March 9th, I learned the meaning of the word "Anschluss," the Annexation of Austria. A few days after the Anschluss, it was my father's job – as mayor of Freilassing – to cross what used to be the German-Austrian border to the neighboring city of Salzburg. With a small entourage of his municipal staff, he drove his convertible Opel across the bridge of the Salzach River into Austria to make a courtesy call to the mayor of Salzburg. Later that evening during dinner, he expressed his bemusement that thousands of Austrians had lined the bridge with raised arms shouting "Heil Hitler!"

Within the following year, looking from the kitchen window onto the distant railroad ramp, I recall seeing prisoners of war being taken from trains and led away. And then, on a cold January morning while eating breakfast, I heard men's voices and the sound of scraping shovels below the window. It had been snowing that night. To find the source of the noise, my mother got up to look out the window. Surprised, she turned toward us to describe that she saw what appeared to be prisoners of war, evidently on detail to clear the snow in front of the mayor's garage.

I rushed to the window to see what a foreign prisoner of war looked like. I had to climb on a chair to look over the edge of the windowsill. There below, on the street, was a small group of men in various types of uniforms shoveling snow while a German soldier, with a rifle hanging loosely from his shoulder, guarded them. As they worked, steam from their breath swirled into the icy morning air. I noticed that some had no mittens, and I worried about their red hands holding the cold shovels. My mother, too, saw how the men repeatedly blew warm steam into their palms. She suddenly left the kitchen and, after a few moments, she came back with several pairs of gloves – among them my brothers' best skiing mittens. She quickly opened the window and, leaning outside into to cold air, she called to the men, "Hello, I have some mittens for you." Surprised, the men looked up, and my mother dropped the mittens out of the window. The men eagerly picked them up and passed them around. A few were still left without mittens, and my mother – being not only resourceful, but imaginative – left the kitchen once more to come back with several heavy wool socks, which she again threw from the window. The men understood and pulled the socks over their red hands. They waved at my mother, and some friendly "danke schoens" followed this brief international exchange.

By September of that year, my father was transferred to Poland to assume the job of civilian administrator of several municipalities under German occupation. These events eventually led to my family spending WWII in Dolzig, (Dolsk) south of Posen, (Poznan).

Freilassing, Railyard

II.
Poland

1939 – 1945

DOLSK 1939

After the Wehrmacht had advanced into Poland in 1939, my father was transferred by the Ministry of Interior from Freilassing – Bavaria, to Dolsk, in Poland. Under civilian administration, this most western province of Poland was named the "Warthegau," after the river Wartha. Now that my reminiscences return to that time, I find it remarkable that I never saw German military occupation forces in the Dolsk area during the five years we lived there. The city of Posen – Poles called it Poznan – was the capital of the province, and located about 40 miles north of Dolsk. Historically, beginning with Frederick the Great during the 18th and later during the 19th century, this area of Poland was part of the Prussian Empire. For this reason, distinct traces of German culture and architecture were prevalent in larger cities like Litzmannstadt, Bromberg and Posen. The latter was endowed with a German university. Because of the Prussian connection, the German minorities were mostly Protestant, and they made up 35 percent of the population. Following the Treaty of Versailles, the province was returned to the Poles, leaving ethnic Germans, the so-called "Volksdeutsche," in a perilous position. These circumstances lead to the notorious Bromberg Bloody Sunday, an incident of atrocities that had taken place on September third, 1939 in the territory referred to as the Polish Corridor, where thousands of ethnic Germans, Volksdeutsche, were killed. Ultimately, as a result of WWII, 15 million Germans were to be expelled from the entire East European area, and two million perished in the course of that agenda.

When we arrived, the town of Dolsk had no electricity, running water, newspaper, hotel, nor a restaurant. There was no firehouse and no hospital, but there was one doctor and a midwife in town. They made their calls in horse-drawn buggies. The only industry was a brick factory in the outskirts of the town, but it was shut down due to scarcity of coal.

A large market square formed the center of town. Its symmetry was shaped by one and two story houses, which looked terribly run-down and in need of paint. City Hall faced the market square, and my father's office was on the second floor. Among the other buildings surrounding the town square was a butcher shop and a bakery; a post office was located on a side street. The town square was dominated by an enormous pump that served as the only source of fresh water for the townspeople. Using the eight foot handle, residents filled their buckets and, to carry them home, they hung one each at the end of a wooden shoulder support. The clatter of horse wagons on the cobblestones was the only traffic. There were no cars.

I can only imagine how my father must have thrown up his hands in view of the task he faced. Since he did not speak Polish, he immediately asked the Polish town elders to select from among themselves his deputy mayor and a management team. He was grateful for their positive response and they became his liaison with the residents of Dolsk. This arrangement was in the interest of not only the town, but also to manage the nineteen rural communities that belonged to the district.

During the first months, I often accompanied my father in his two-horse Landau when he surveyed the surroundings. We discovered breathtaking scenery. The town's southern perimeter was met by the shore of a beautiful lake. Unfortunately, the run-down condition of houses and ramshackle backyards, with tall weeds and broken fences, spoiled the shoreline. A long row of hills, crowned with forests, surrounded Dolsk. They emerged from areas of large wetlands, from reeds and brown peat bogs alongside the lake.

The appearance of the nineteen villages that belonged to the district of Dolsk showed great poverty. Dilapidated farm buildings with animal waste seeping from stables, and dwellings with dim windows and eye-level eaves made up the small communities. Often, the dirt road leading through the village ended at the gates of a magnificent manse inside a park setting. These large estates dated back to the feudal days of the Polish aristocracy, whose vast land holdings were worked by tenant farmers.

After our furniture arrived from Germany, my mother tried to again create the comfortable home we were used to. She first turned one of the many rooms into a music salon, where she placed her Boesendorfer grand piano. The house had no central heating – instead, each room contained either a fireplace or a glazed tile stove. My mother chose as our everyday living room one that was smaller and close to the kitchen wing. It featured a porcelain tile stove, the ornate top almost reached the ceiling and an uphol-

1939, a village in the district of Dolsk, south of Poznan.

Dolsk, town section, facing the lake.

stered bench surrounded it. Above the door for fuel, the stove had a small opening with a decorative hinged brass door just large enough to keep coffee hot or slowly bake an apple, which might take an entire afternoon, but made the room smell wonderful.

To begin our new lives my mother had to make important adjustments in her everyday care of the family. Because of the high risk of typhoid in the area – vaccinations or antibiotics were not yet available – our drinking water had to be boiled. Despite these precautions, during the first year Ernst and I did come down with the disease. It took several weeks before we recovered our strength.

Other changes we had to get used to mostly concerned the food. Without a grocery store, our food came directly from its sources, such as milk which was brought from the farm – the same with eggs and chickens. The cook bought the flour and grain products from a nearby mill. The everyday use of water to flush the toilets and to use the only water heater in one of the bathrooms, was supplied by a large reservoir in the attic, which was kept full by pumping water at least once a week for ten minutes with a lever that was mounted in the kitchen hall. The lack of electricity taught us the use of candles and petroleum lamps.

At the time, I was only nine years old and did not quite comprehend the significance of a monument that I discovered across the street from our gate. It consisted of a plaque, mounted inside a recessed wall. Cast in bronze, it listed the names of 38 ethnic Germans, residents of Dolsk, who had been massacred following the outbreak of the war. The details of the atrocity terrified me: the story that the victims' tongues were nailed to the table, and the case of mutilation of a German farmer whose legs were chopped off in front of his wife and children before they, too, were murdered. The memorial had been erected only a few weeks before we arrived…

BROMBERG MASSACRE – POLAND 1939

*A **German pastor praying over victims.***

Massenhaft erschlagene und erschossene Volksdeutsche vor Warschau. Verstreut an Straßen, auf Feldern und in Wäldern. Aufgefundene werden am Sammelort rekognosziert. **Translation:** *Bromberg mass murder of ethnic Germans, September 3, 1939 when thousands were beaten to death or shot.* **Shown:** *piles of corpses gathered for identification. Bromberg's "Bloody Sunday" is an event that took place in and around Bydgiszca (German "Bromberg"), the territory referred to as the Polish Corridor. "…After the invasion of Poland by German forces in 1939, thousands of ethnic Germans were collected by the Polish authorities from a number of cities and towns and sent on a march, herded from town to town. Some sources claim over 60,000 Germans were murdered – including many pastors, precisely because they were the 'official link' to the ethnic Germans."*
(Ian Kershaw: Hitler: Nemesis 1936-1945; Jon Toland: Adolf Hitler)

MY FATHER'S MICROPHONE

The problems in the small town of Dolsk were over-whelming. To deal with them, however, my father brought with him two enormous talents. One, he was a great communicator; the other, he was an organizer. His job in Dolsk called for both.

Without electricity, a newspaper, or radio, his gift of communications would have been useless, if he had not been also innovative. He used a car battery to operate a public address system. For this purpose he had a small platform set up in front of City Hall facing the market square, and via a microphone he addressed the people of the town. He did this whenever he announced a new pro-ject. It was helpful that the majority of Poles in this area spoke German – but he still used an interpreter at these occasions.

The first of these messages was a call for volunteers to bring their own shovels and other tools and meet the next Saturday at the cemetery, which needed cleaning up. The cemetery was located on a beautiful hill beside the lake, but it was a wilderness of overgrowth and years of ne-glect. A surprisingly large number of men showed up the following Saturday with rakes and shovels over their shoulders; and women brought flowering plants to adorn graves. The project was successful, and people seemed pleased.

With the German occupation of Poland, the Szloty had lost its value, which actually didn't matter much because people in Dolsk hadn't worked for a salary in years and poverty was rampant. In this connection his next message, again over his public address system, was that from now on salaries will be paid in form of Reichsmarks, and every resident will have a savings book waiting for him in the new bank which, during his administration, had opened at the town square.

Dolsk, (DOLZIG in German) Warthegau 1941, after my father's
beautification program of the town square. The old Town Water Pump
at right of flowerbed with the City Hall wall at left edge of photo (left).
View from city hall (right).

In early spring, my father announced that the town had purchased paint, free for the residents, so that they can paint the houses that faced the town square. Next, he informed the people that the municipal workshop had built flowerboxes, that are ready to be picked up, and that plants would be supplied by the town's nursery.

Soon, the old city stables and yards were rehabilitated and filled with work horses. Old wagons and equipment were repaired and men and foremen were hired to run the stables, operate a working farm and a nursery. On surrounding hills a vineyard, berry bog and huge orchards soon became my father's main undertakings. The result was that by the fall of his first two years in office, the hills surrounding Dolsk were planted with 280.000 fruit trees. Another project was the building of greenhouses on municipal land. I recall my father taking visiting officials on tour to show with special pride the greenhouses' novel heating systems, which one of the Polish gardeners had designed.

One day, he had a very special announcement for the community – that's after he had obtained from the German government a generator for the town's defunct power station. However, due to rationing, he lacked enough black coal needed to fire it up, unless the residents volunteered to turn over their anthracite rations to the city. In exchange he offered to replace the rations with plentiful brown coal and all the peat they needed from the bogs surrounding the lake, for cooking and for their parlor stoves. The response was sufficient so that, within a year, Dolsk had electric power during several hours each day.

When my father originally saw Dolsk – the lake and the natural beauty of the surroundings – he made plans to turn the community into a tourist resort. Again, for this reason, the town needed to employ people to clean up the lake shore and to renovate several abandoned mansions, turning them into guest houses and a tourist inn. The rundown beach area was landscaped, and one of the shabby buildings was restored and turned into a terrace restaurant that faced the lake. To create water activities, the city bought two sailboats, several paddle boats and a couple of water bikes. It was not long before busloads of tourists arrived from the Reich and from Polish cities, bringing business and employment.

Later (the year must have been 1942), with government support, my father built a community center that contained

Public Beach Party, 1942 (left). Ernst, friend and Murrax (right).

an auditorium. There, a screen was installed and, with the new source of electricity, Dolsk residents eventually could – for the first time – watch movies. I recall that the cellar of this building also served to store large blocks of ice that were cut from the lake during the long Polish winters and were laid on piles of sawdust. Without refrigeration anywhere, this was the only place in town that residents could store perishables – from meats and venison, to fish and eggs.

My father's efforts of turning uncultivated acres that surrounded Dolsk into productive land use began to pay off when, by 1942, large tandem trucks from Poznan and Chemnitz arrived in Dolsk to pick up watermelons, rhubarb, crates of berries, and loads of sunflowers and poppies, that could be refined into cooking oils.

These efforts converted Dolsk into a town where the natives, Polish workers, became "indispensable" during Germany's all-out war efforts. It meant that when my father received requests to send Poles to the Reich for the defense industry, he was able to declare their status as "indispensable" in the production of food. Naturally, the residents appreciated that their family members did not need to leave. Conversely, it was interesting that some Poles – mostly singles and unemployed in the surrounding communities – actually chose to go to Germany to work on farms and industry in order to benefit from better living conditions.

In 1941, his architectural office designed a new housing development on one of the hills. I remember it well, because Ernst, as a first year architectural student at the University of Poznan, did his internship in that office under the supervision of the town's architect by the name of "Okay." He was the first person I ever met who had lived many years in America. Of course, now I wonder how he ever ended up with a name like Okay. At the time, nobody in Germany had ever heard that word before, nor understood its meaning...

To keep as many agricultural employees occupied as possible during the winter, my father turned the municipal workshop into a place for making wood products, such as built-in bunk beds and doors for the new housing units. Lathes and other machines were installed, and workers, who tended the fields and orchards in the summer, made furniture, trays, bowls, candlesticks, and similar items in the winter. Other workers repaired greenhouses, built new flowerboxes, and assembled the espalier and support for the vineyards. After years of economic coma, the people of Dolsk actually worked, saved money, and did not have to leave the town, under the ever-increasing pressure generated by WWII, to send defense workers to Germany.

As a result of my father's judicious treatment of the area's people under occupation and extreme wartime stress, the Poles were decent when later, in 1945, we Germans were vulnerable and forced to flee from the advancing Soviets. I can't forget that they could have harmed us. In fact, my father's Polish assistant wanted to leave with him. After our departure in 1945, Dolsk was left with a favorable German legacy.

In the 1980s while living in New England, I met visitors from Dolsk, who described the town as a prosperous community with a major canning industry, thanks to the large orchards that my father had created. And, because of his initiative, Dolsk by the lake is, today, a well-known Polish resort that can be found on tourist brochures – and on the Internet.

DOLSK – MY FATHER'S GOOD WORKS:

Dolsk – 1943, lake activities and the new Community Center, large brick building, left of center.

Beach promenade, 1945: My father planned every park bench, flowerbed, and tree-rose along the path. At the end of the path, the steep gable of the kitchen building of our residence is visible.

Today's view from what was my father's office, exhibiting his original landscaping in front of city hall – the town square, as found in current tourist brochures and on the Internet.

THE PASSING OF SEASONS
Reminiscence of my Childhood in Poland.

It is the first day of summer vacation with no more school to pattern my days – to keep me from playing the wonderful game that only I know of, the game that moves me away from where everyone else is. I will leave them all behind when I move back to my island, to the memories of last summer. It will be just as it was on Robison Crusoe's Island. The story was so wonderful, and all last summer I did everything the way the book described – and I want to go back to where Robinson Crusoe is.

I had a twig hut and I ate berries from the raspberry bushes. I shot apples from the trees with my bow and arrow, and I baked potatoes in a coal pit. I shared my Robinson Crusoe island with Frederika the goat. Murrax, my wire terrier, had no special role; he was just there – and so was Mars, the St. Bernard, and Felix, the huge gray rabbit with his fat goiter and floppy ears that dragged on the ground.

I first have to find the circular twig hut. I run along the gravel path to get to the hidden cove beyond the tall hazelnut bushes. This reminds me: I also cracked and ate the hazelnuts last summer when I was Robinson Crusoe. I shuffle through some dead branches and underbrush until I reach the small clearing and find the remains of Robinson Crusoe's twig hut. The branches I had pushed into the ground last summer still stand in a circle.

Lush foliage which I had woven through the upright branches now looks dry and brittle, and part of the roof has dropped into the hut by the weight of last winter's snow. I lift the end of the roof and fit it back onto the supporting branches – there is so much work to be done! I crawl into the hut and examine it from the inside. Well, it is much smaller than it was last summer, and I can see through the walls and the roof; all around me are holes! With my hands, I rake up some damp leaves and throw them outside through the entrance. This place needs cleaning!

I return to Crusoe's twig hut every day and weave long willow branches and other foliage through the supporting branches. I even find raspberry stakes to reinforce the walls and to hold the roof. Murrax, Mars and Dina – the new girl Saint Bernard – crawl into the hut with me, and there we sit. No one can see us.

I go over to the stables and get the goat. Frederika is the only brown goat among the herd of white Saanen goats. She is really not a very nice-looking goat, but she's the only one I am allowed to play with. Frederika has a sway back and a huge stomach and, underneath, she has a routine udder. Her cheeks always stick out on each side while her jaw moves in a circular rhythm chewing cud. It gives her a look of blasé preoccupation. Her horns are what make Frederika distinct from the other goats, who don't have any. Hers are beautiful, ribbed, curved and large like two handles – and I can grab them and hold her. Frederika has light amber eyes with black horizontal slits, she has a silky beard, and she eats everything.

I find her collar and a rope. From there we go to pick up Felix, the Belgian Giant rabbit. We reach the long row of three-story rabbit hutches full of fluffy Angoras, Blue Seals and Chinchilla Silvers. I am looking for Felix with his floppy ears. There he is!

I lift him out of the hutch – he must weigh thirty pounds this year – what a champion! I have to scold Murrax because he barks at Felix. He calms down when I let him sniff Felix and I talk to him persuasively, telling him not to scare Felix. Dina and Mars don't care about rabbits; they only look Felix over with their bloodshot, droopy Saint Bernard eyes.

With Frederika on a rope, Felix in my arms, and the three dogs around, I make my way through the garden back to the twig hut. First thing is to put Felix on the ground. He will stay in the same spot all day, munching grass like an eating machine whereas, for Frederika, I must find the stake I used last summer to tie her up – far enough away from the twig hut, because she eats everything. Last summer she ate a picture book, Robinson Crusoe's sun umbrella and my watercolor kit.

So now I crawl inside the twig hut. The dogs follow me. I tell Mars to sit down – it is too tight in here – and I shout at Dina to get out of the doorway, she shuts out the light. And here we sit in Robinson Crusoe's twig hut. No one can see us.

There is something missing. Oh dear, I forgot "Gockl," the Plymouth Rock hen. I tie up the dogs and run to get Gockl. She is what might be called a soup hen – gray-striped, very large with a low abdomen, a tiny red comb on her head, and canary-yellow feet.

When I reach the chicken yard, there are so many striped Plymouth Rocks that I'm confused. "Gockl, Gockl – Gockl?" It's hard to tell. I go into the shed and pick up an empty grain sack. If I can't find Gockl, I shall never know what happened to her! She remembers the Robinson Crusoe days of last summer; she clucks and hesitantly comes toward my hand." Gockl, Gockl?" and she starts to eat from my palm. I quickly throw the burlap sack over her. There is some ado and screeching as I fold the sack around her. I carry her off and she calms down. I set her down in front of the hut and show her the scattered barley and the dish of water.

Things are getting just the way they were last summer and I am very busy. I have to make another bow and arrow – I can't find the old one. Like Robinson Crusoe, we'll go hunting. I first strap two square garden baskets, one on each side of Dina's back – she is my llama – and then we all walk to the orchard. With my bow and arrow, I miss several times before I succeed in shooting down some apples.

I put them into Dina's baskets, but she keeps sitting down and I have to scold her because the apples keep rolling out. Those apples are really sour, but Frederika will eat them.

I have all kinds of things in my twig hut. There is the jack knife with three blades – one blade is broken – then several bowls and an enamel pot. I have a shovel and a harmonica, but every time I play it, Murrax will not stop howling. I also have a mat to sleep on, a small stool, some carrots – Felix loves them – and for the dogs I have some smoked salami from the kitchen, which I mix with bread pieces – they don't know this – it smells all the same to them. I assign to each a bowl and they cooperate well.

Everyone seems very happy. Felix just sits and eats, his ears lying on the ground beside him, Gockl stays around her barley. She doesn't lay eggs – she never did last summer, – maybe that's why she is a soup hen. Frederika is the significant one in this arrangement because she has to be milked. Antek showed me how to do that last summer.

I put the enamel saucepan under her stomach; while I talk to her nicely. Frederika holds still, and – swish, swish – I fill the pan. But then, before I can get up, she grabs my pigtail and yanks it, and I have to scream at her. Just like Robinson Crusoe, I drink some of the warm milk and give the rest to the dogs because I don't want to make cheese anyway.

Everything works very well. The sun shines on Robinson Crusoe's twig hut, and I sit inside and look outside. It smells so good of earth and leaves – the hut is wonderful and secret. And no one can see me.

So what has to be done next? I don't want to look for berries again – this morning I noticed they had worms. The bow doesn't seem as taut as it was last summer, I can't find the right string and, actually, I hope no one sees me shooting apples with a bow and arrow.

By late afternoon, I have to milk Frederika again. Frankly, this summer Frederika has an unpleasant odor, she smells like a goat. I look at Mars and Dina. It is warm and their tongues hang out and they drool. Felix just sits and eats with his ears spread on the ground, and he is very boring; and Gockl does not know the difference where she is. I have a wristwatch – last year I didn't – and I just remember that I have a piano lesson at four and I have to change clothes and practice first. Last year I did not have piano lessons yet.

I sit in my twig hut with Murrax on my lap, I look around me at the wilting leaves on the walls. No one can see me. Oh, Robinson Crusoe…

LOTS OF PETS

My daily activities were filled with animals. I had more animals than any one I ever knew the rest of my life, from horses, fallow deer, raccoons, peacocks, to foxes inside a run with dens, and an aviary with squirrels and fantail doves. Even the number of dogs around me as a child was extraordinary. At one time we had 13 dogs – I guess it was at a moment that the number included a litter by one of them. Anyway, my mother had a silky Dachshund and an elegant Setter, and my father had hunting dogs – a couple of Short-haired Pointers. But there were several more, among them two Saint Bernards, Dina and Mars, who just laid around in the drive inside the iron gates and, one year, my father added a Siberian Sled Dog to the kennel menagerie. It was a breed that was very rare in Europe at the time and, as I was told, Siberian Sled Dogs were closest related to wolves, which explained why this female Sled Dog couldn't bark – she only emitted long mournful howls. I learned to dislike her intensely when I found out one day that she had eaten her new litter of puppies. Another memorable dog was my father's specially-trained Schutzhund, which he had shipped from Berlin. This massive gray German Shepherd was turned loose every night inside my father's locked office at city-hall. "Thor" was to serve as special security, and I was told to stay away from him, because he was so dangerous that even the caretaker used a rake with a long handle in order to push the bowl of food within reach. This danger intrigued me very much, considering that all the other dogs were my friends. And soon, on a sunny afternoon, I secretly took Thor off the chain and we went down to the lake to play. I threw rocks into the water, and he ran like a fool to stick his head under the water to retrieve the rock, and when he bounded back to the shore he knocked me down jumping all over me, delighted that he had finally found a playmate. Later, I tied him back up in front of his house. At dinner that evening, I found out that somebody had already reported my escapade with Thor to my father. These circumstances led to my father's great anger. Firstly – I was told with a raised voice – I could have been hurt playing with a dog that was ex-tremely dangerous. Secondly, the dog was trained NOT to play with children, but to attack trespassers or to defend against attackers; and, thirdly, by my chumming with this attack dog, I was ruining his special training – the very qualifications that my father had paid good money for when he had Thor shipped from Berlin. From then on I left Thor alone – because I was obedient.

Actually, it was Murrax, my wire terrier, who was the most important among all the dogs. None of the others ever achieved his rank. From the time I got Murrax at age six – while we still lived in Freilassing – I considered him a sibling. At night, he slept in the small of my knees un-der my bed cover, and he allowed me to stuff him into my doll carriage anytime. I didn't care for dolls, even though I had a celluloid doll that remained nameless in my memory. There is no question, while in Poland – having few other children to play with – it was Murrax who was my best friend, and he always was by my side everywhere I went. He got all my attention because – in contrast to plastic dolls – he responded like a real live pal. We understood each other perfectly and, for this reason, we also had terrible fights when he got furious, flashed his teeth, barked and sometimes, at the pique of his rage, he would even bite me, leaving welts on my thumb so that I slapped him – only to cuddle him quickly to make up. That's how it was.

HORSE–CRAZY

By the time summer vacation started, I had made a number of friends among my new classmates. Most of them were Volksdeutsche, the ethnic German minority group who had lived in Poland for many generations. For this reason, their German language was flavored with a heavy Slavic accent.

Hedwig Schimanski was one of my new friends. She wore her blond hair in a blunt haircut at shoulder length, and sometimes she wore a wilted taffeta ribbon that held a strand of hair on one side of her head. Hedwig had scabies between her knuckles which sometimes cracked and bled – and I was always careful not to touch her hands.

Although it smelled a lot, I loved to visit Hedwig's farm with the big manure pile in the middle of the yard and chickens scratching on top of it. I liked her farm mostly because I could be with her horses when they plowed or pulled a wagon or a mower. At the end of the day, I rode them home from the field. Other times, I first drove the horses with the wagon right into the lake to let them cool their feet. Often, I helped to unhitch them. It was especially thrilling when I stretched high to pull the harnesses over their heads and then lead the large animals to the water trough, where I watched them dip their muzzles deep into the water, their flaring nostrils barely clearing the surface. Afterwards, I took them to their stalls and helped feed them. Often I curried the horses' flanks and necks, and I was pleased when they obediently lifted their hooves for me to inspect the nails that held their iron shoes. There was so much to learn about horses. I liked the way they held their ears in different positions indicating their mood at the moment, and I found their manes and tail hair beautiful – some were wavy. And they did not seem to mind at all when I turned up their velvety lips to marvel at their large brown teeth. How accommodating they were when I asked them to move over so that I could squeeze between them – they were actually polite. I loved horses, and they smelled wonderful.

Inside Hedwig's stucco farmhouse, the kitchen was dark and steamy because, on the peat stove, there was usually a large zinc kettle full of boiling potatoes. After they cooled, Hedwig mashed them with a large wooden paddle and then she poured some whey over them to thin the mass. Later, I helped her mix scoops of bran into the warm and squishy potato mixture which I stirred with my bare hands. Nobody there scolded me for getting my hands dirty all the way up to my armpits. Finally, I helped pour buckets of the soupy potatoes into the pigs' troughs. They pushed each other and made me want to cheer them on as their lusty squeals drowned into gurgling, smacking sounds with their snouts sunk deep into the warm swill.

Then one day when I visited Hedwig, she was crying because her grandmother had died the night before. I had seen her grandmother only once. I remembered that she wore wooden clogs, a long skirt and a black babushka, and her mouth seemed collapsed into a thin line under the nose. I don't think she had any teeth. The house was very quiet when Hedwig lead me into the parlor where I had never been before. The curtains were drawn, and the room was very dark so that it took my eyes a moment to adjust after coming from the bright sun outside. I finally recognized the small figure lying on the floor. There was a mound of sawdust under the sheet where Hedwig's grandmother was lying. Her dead hands held a crucifix, and a candle was burning by each side of her head.

That afternoon, Hedwig and I rode with her father to the other end of town on a potato wagon to pick up a casket from the carpenter. I was so proud when Hedwig's father handed me the reins. He must have noticed that I had learned to allow the necessary space to maneuver both horses and wagon around turns, because I no longer got stuck driving the team through the narrow gate of his farmyard and, in town, I turned street corners without getting on the sidewalk. Crossing the market square, the horses' hooves clopped and the wagon rumbled noisily on the cobble stones. With apprehension, I looked up to the windows of my father's office in City Hall, hoping that he would not happen to look outside to see me on the potato cart with the casket for Hedwig's grandmother.

Soon it was August and, one evening, my father asked me to stay at the table after dinner. He wanted to talk to me. He seemed unusually moved when he began to tell me that Frau von Goeschel, a close friend of our family, had visited him at the office earlier that day. She had come to explain that, a few weeks before her husband's sudden death, he had bought a small horse from one of the tenant farmers and, because it was underfed, he had kept it for a while in his stable in order to bring it back to good health.

That's how I learned that the baron had seen me drive through town a team of horses that pulled a potato wagon with a casket, which made him think that I desperately needed my own horse. For this reason, when he happened to find the small mare, he decided that she would be just right for me. Now, after the baron had died, the widow had come to inform my father that the small horse was ready to be turned over, to be mine...

wwwwwwwwwwwwwwwwwwww

LIESL

After school, on the day of my tenth birthday, my father had come home from the office to show me my new pony. There she was – dark brown with a thick black mane, her tail had wavy long hair, and she had white socks on her hind legs. I gave my father a big hug and jumped up and down with excitement. This was my own horse. I no longer had to go to Hedwig's farm to be near her big plow horses, just so I could harness them, to water them, to ride the team to the field or, like the time we drove her potato wagon across town, to pick up her grandmother's casket from the carpenter.

My new pony was a girl – just like myself – and she was small, perfectly custom-sized for me. In fact, her eyes were at the level of my own. They were a beautiful dark amber with long lashes right there before my face. She had a soft velvety muzzle and she smelled so good. I pried her jaws apart to check her teeth, just like Antek the horseman did – it was from watching his ways that I had learned to tell a horse's age. By examining the brown oblong markings on the blunt top of her teeth I gathered that my new pony was my own age. Without thinking about it carefully, I called her Liesl. I don't know why I chose that name, but it sounded friendly to me – and Liesl was going to be my friend.

That evening, I rushed through dinner because I had to get back to the stables while it was still daylight. There I put oats into Liesl's trough so that she would not have to

With friends, my first ride on Liesl (left). Liesl and I, wishing for a saddle! (right)

eat so much hay. Hay gives horses big bellies, whereas oats makes horses sleek and gives them a shiny coat. I opened another bail of straw for her bedding so that she would be warm. In the adjacent stable where the large work horses were kept, I looked for a curry iron and comb and I groomed Liesl for a long time. She began to nuzzle me in return. I think before I finally left the stable, I kissed her good night on her forehead.

Next morning I woke at dawn and, before I had to leave for school, I rushed to the stables. I still could not believe that I had this new pony all to myself, and I wanted to check how Liesl had slept. When I opened her stall I found her lying on her side on the soft straw. That's when I did something I had never done before with a horse – I sat down between her stretched-out bony legs. She raised her head and looked a little un-easy, because horses feel defenseless while lying down, and usually scramble to their feet when a person approaches. But I noticed that Liesl seemed relaxed while I sat close to her. It was almost like sitting next to Dina, our St. Bernard. Eventually, Liesl got up and I ran to bring her some water, and she dipped her muzzle deep into the pail.

After school, I again rushed to the stable and I put a bridle and bits on Liesl for the first time to lead her outside. That's when I became painfully aware that I had no saddle for her. It was war time and a saddle was hard to come by, especially one of the size for a pony.

In the meantime, Antek helped me get on Liesl's bare back, at least to ride her across the courtyard. Liesl, being unaccustomed to her new environment, seemed a little skittish and, without a saddle, I felt insecure on her slippery back. I was surprised that I suddenly felt afraid of Liesl. After all, she was considerably bigger than I and she wore those iron horseshoes – but she probably was afraid of me too.

〜〜〜〜〜〜〜〜〜〜〜

IT'S REALLY A CINCH

There is one part of my life where I can't remember eating breakfast, washing my hair, or paying much attention to what I wore or how I looked. That was a time when I probably looked terrible. I think I had a braided pigtail over each ear. I remember I was not fond of taking baths, preferring to go swimming in the lake, and I recall wearing sandals and straight cut frocks without a slip or a waistline. I was not interested in being a girl or what girls do, or what they are supposed to play with. I do remember having a celluloid doll, which I got for Christmas – however she remained unnamed and I never saw her again after the day I made room in the doll carriage for Murrax, my terrier. He allowed me to even tie a bonnet on his scruffy head, but he put up a terrible fight squirming, growling and flashing his teeth at me furiously when I attempted to lay him on his back on the doll's pillow so that I could push him around the yard in the carriage.

Since I had gotten Liesl, my main goal each morning was to rush out of the house to get to the stables. Liesl had her own stall, separate from the large horses. I cautiously got acquainted with her. Having had "horse experiences" with large work horses only, I now had to switch my thinking from "huge" to "pony-size." Where in the past I could barely reach the bridle bit on large horses, Liesl was small enough so that I could put my arms over her back. In the past, I had to climb on something like a fence rail or a wagon and then have somebody lead the horse sideways in front of me, before I could even get my legs over the back. But with Liesl all this was going to be much easier – once I got a saddle with stirrups. Then I finally would be able to try out my new pony – to check her gait, her responses to the rein and her general temperament. I was actually a little uneasy about Liesl...

With the shortage of most anything because of the war, it was difficult to find a saddle for a normal-sized horse, and it was nearly impossible to get a pony-size saddle. A few times I cautiously rode Liesl bareback with my feet dangling helplessly at her sides, or I led her around the yard trying to teach her to follow me. I fed and watered her, curried her fur, or sat in the straw next to her when she was lying down. Mostly, I just loved to look at her.

Liesl was beautiful with her thick black mane and a white star between her eyes. She had a very long tail, the tips of the wavy hair nearly dragging on the ground. She seemed too narrow in the chest and her knee joints were a little too large, which I understood was the result of rickets, poor feeding from early age – when she was still a filly. As was customary among farmers in Poland, often a mare was hitched to a cart or a plow while her foal trotted alongside, going through the same distances and routines as the mother. Who knows? Perhaps this was the reason Liesl had rickets when, during her childhood, she did not have enough time or occasions to get her fill of milk as she trotted along while her mother worked. Owning Liesl, I found that there were so many worries! At least I was sure that, being my pony now, Liesl would always be well-fed.

Without hope of getting a real saddle soon, I began to think of how to make some kind of improvisations that would make a substitute. Remembering that next to the carriage house was a tackle room, and there, hanging on the wall, I found some dusty harnesses. Among them, there was one that looked small, and I even found some old rusty stirrups on a shelf. I dissembled most of the parts – leaving only the cinch – and, with a few modifications, I managed to attach the stirrups. I used a folded blanket to create a saddlecloth which I placed under the cinch and -- that was it! I had all the necessary components that make up the closest semblance of a saddle. It certainly would be an improvement over riding Liesl's slippery, bare back. Now, with the stirrups, my feet would no longer hang by her sides without support – in addition, I could hold on to the cinch, if needed.

It was shortly before the Harvest Festival when my father told me one morning that there had been an accident and that Liesl was sick. She had walked behind one of the large horses in the stalls and was kicked, causing a rupture in her flank. I was warned that I must not ride her for a while. I cried and ran to the stable where I found Liesl with a wide bandage wrapped around her stomach. Antek tried to explain, "She'll be alright, Fraulein," he said. "The veterinarian will operate and fix it." He then hurried away. The following days I spent my entire free time sitting next to Liesl on the straw. I fed her carrots and scratched her ears.

That's when one morning my mother surprised me with the announcement that we will go on a trip for a few days. She said good bye to my father, and our suitcases were already waiting in the hall. We took a train to Munich to visit Aunt Lilly, and brought her some special black current preserves and a smoked eel.

When we returned from our trip – Liesl's stall was empty…

Liesl, injured by a large horse. Bandage around flanks is visible in the background.

A "GOATS" STORY

During summer vacation, I began to pay attention to the goats. This led me to walk to the farmyard early one morning so that I would be there when Antek took the herd to pasture. I stood waiting for them to come out, and after he opened the stable door I was stunned by a cloud of dense odor that emptied upon me like from an immense, invisible bag. The acrid smell wafted around my head and almost pushed me to my knees. I knew that goat bucks create this terrible odor. It comes from their yellow, sticky beard which they drench for reasons of unspeakable rituals with a stream of urine, while lowering the head toward their flanks…

As the goats scrambled by me on their way to the outside, I tried to ease my discomfort by holding my breath as long as I could, and I was relieved that after a few gasps my sense of smell had turned numb from the exotic stench. I began to focus on what I had come for. Since Liesl, my beloved pony had died the previous fall, I thought of the big goat buck to take her place. He was almost as tall in the shoulders as the pony had been. At first he ran by me with the herd and nearly got away before I grabbed him by the neck from behind, and for a moment I had to wrestle with him to slow him down. During some hectic doings, I finally managed to grab a fistful of his sticky yellow beard, holding him long enough to slip a collar on his neck. From there I took him over to the tackle room by the horse stables, where I tried to fit him with Liesl's harness. I soon realized, however, that he was built totally different than Liesl. His chest was much too narrow for the harness and it kept sliding off. Besides, he was extremely unruly. Even though he was the type of goat buck that had no horns, he still used his head to butt me from all directions, and he kept stepping on my toes while he struggled against me. His untamed behaviour finally convinced me that he probably would never cooperate with my intentions to hitch him to a cart. In the end I was glad to give up, and I took him back to Antek and the herd.

Later, going home for lunch, I entered the house when I ran into Wanda in the hall. As I came near her, she looked at me startled, and then she threw her arms up in the air and let out a long shriek. She walked around me holding her nose, and with a shrill voice she told me not to move and to wait while she ran to call my mother. Anyway, there was a flurry of activities and cries of "ugh" and disgust and "phooeys," while my clothes were being taken off right there in the hall. And then they put me in the tub – even before it was filled with water...

MY NEW PIANO TEACHER!

It all began in Freilassing. I was five years old when I became a piano pupil of Fraulein Deeg of the Mozarteum Conservatory in Salzburg. She used the "Bisping Rose Method," which was preparatory for the study of classical piano music. Fraulein Deeg was a formidable woman and very pleasant when she ushered me into her studio for my weekly one-hour lesson. Before she sat down next to me at the piano, she seemed to follow a ritual of first filling with fresh water a pewter tumbler that was embossed in heraldic images, from which she sipped intermittently throughout the lesson. Being so young when I began, all I remember of my first piano lessons is Fraulein Deeg's pewter tumbler. Yet without her I would probably have never learned parallel scales and arpeggios.

In 1939 I was eight and, having moved to Poland, I longed to resume piano lessons without delay but, for nearly two years, I could not find a teacher. It was only through coincidence that I learned about the von Sanke family. Originally from Latvia, they lived on an estate about ten kilometers from Dolsk. Mr. and Mrs. von Sanke's daughter was a professor at the Berlin Academy of Music, and she regularly spent both her summer vacation and Christmas holidays with her parents in Poland. I was more than ready when my mother relayed the happy news that Asta, the daughter was willing to teach me, whenever she came from Berlin.

It was clear that in order to reach the Seehof, the von Sanke estate, I had to go by horseback. Since Liesl, my pony had died the previous summer, my father had acquired two teams of Panje horses, Russian draft ponies; and, of these four horses, my favorite became a chestnut mare because of her even temperament. I called her "Perle." She was a little larger than Liesl and, in comparison to Liesl's dainty hooves, Perle's were large and flat and, when she trotted, she was terribly bumpy under the saddle. The ups-and-downs loosened my hair beret and made my teeth clatter, if I didn't clench them. But I was getting used to her.

I was very excited the afternoon when I saddled Perle to ride to the Seehof for my first piano lesson. I tied my book bag to the saddle and took off. After passing the last houses of Dolsk with the loud clop-clop of Perle's flat hooves on the cobble stones, I arrived at the ridge of hills that surrounded Dolsk, located in a valley by the side of the beautiful lake. As I rode down the other side of the hill, leaving

Dolsk behind, a dusty road replaced the cobblestones. I suddenly realized how alone I was on top of my horse. I had never before ridden outside of Dolsk. I saw neither people nor any traffic on the road; in fact, there were few cars in Poland during WWII.

Although my father had a small DKW, (pronounced "de kah way"), he seldom used it. DKW stood for "Deutscher Kraft Wagen." Because of the DKWs' flimsy construction, Germans nicknamed them "de-kah-whoopdies." I must hasten to add that, after WWII, the de-kah-whoopdies eventually developed into the respectable "Audi." The reason my father only rarely drove his de-kah-whoopdie, was that there were no gas stations. Besides, most roads, not being blacktopped, were deeply rutted and impassable for automobiles during bad weather. That's why almost everyone in Poland traveled by horseback or carriage.

I remembered that I had to look for a sign on the left side of the road with the words "Seehof." After a few kilometers I began to worry that I might have missed the turn, and I noticed that the road ahead of me led into an invisible horizon without a house in sight. Suddenly, frightening thoughts flashed through my mind. What if Perle were to throw me and run away, and I would lay there in the dust? Because I was not expected to be back home until late afternoon, nobody would even look for me. With increasing uneasiness I scanned the roadside for the sign and, finally, there it was.

I kicked Perle in the flank with the heels of my sandals to motivate her into her bone-shaking canter. In the distance, I saw a wooded area but, still, no houses. To my relief, when I approached the edge of the cluster of stately oaks, I found an open wrought-iron gate. Two graceful Gordon Setters greeted me as I followed the groomed gravel path through a park to the entrance of an ancient mansion. I tied up Perle and took my music bag off the saddle. Just then, an attractive young woman stepped from the door and, extending her hand, she greeted me: "Guten Tag,

*Russian Draft Pony – "Perle" after school on to piano lessons (left).
"Bobby & Teddy" and horse cart with cousin Renate, "Murrax" and his
son, "Batzi" (right).*

Gudrun. So nice to meet you." I was thrilled to have finally
found not only a piano teacher, but she also was the most
beautiful lady I had ever seen in Poland. "Very nice to meet
you, Miss von Sanke" I said, and I curtsied when I shook her
hand. She put her arm over my shoulder and led me
through a large foyer into the salon to a Boesendorfer grand
piano, the same as my mother's. Without delay, I unpacked
my music books so that she could assess my level of studies.
That afternoon, Asta von Sanke introduced me to my first
Schubert Impromptu. Subsequently, for three years during
summer vacations and Christmas Holidays, often when
snow drifts reached Perle's belly, I made my way to Seehof,
just to get a few piano lessons whenever Asta von Sanke had
come from Berlin to Poland.

THE BOARDING SCHOOL

I began high school in 1941, in occupied Poland. At the
time, the civilian administration set up a few schools that
were based on the German educational system which, to
this day, consists of eight years of high school and which, for
this reason, begins at the age of ten for the student. For me,
the nearest high school was in Srem, the district city about

twelve kilometers from where I lived. It was a boarding school for boys with the specific intent to accommodate the sons of what was then the German elite of the Nazi period. As a result, many of these offspring were sons of aristocrats, often referred to as "Junkers," of field grade officers, and also of industrialists, as well as scientists and diplomats of the Third Reich.

Being located in Poland, the school also served to keep the boys out of harm's way during the bombing of German cities. As a girl, I needed special permission to attend this school – which eventually led to the oddity that I was the only girl among six hundred cadets in blue uniforms during those first few months.

Since there was no means of transportation where we lived, I had to commute by carriage the first year I attended the school in Srem. My father ordered that the town's stables were to provide the carriage, a team of horses and Frantek, the horseman, for the daily 30 kilometer roundtrip. In addition to myself, there were eventually four other girls from Dolsk who joined me. In the winter, we often traveled in a sleek black sled, where we girls kept warm under fur blankets. That's when the horses' snorting, the muffled sound of their hooves on the snow, and the squeaking of their leather harnesses shattered the winter morning's frosty silence. And the fresh snow chirped under the sleds' iron runners. Often we broke a trail because, at such an early hour, no one else had yet been on the road before us.

Because of the school's unique student body, some of the boys' names that I still remember, took on added significance only after I matriculated from childhood into adulthood through the torturous years of World War II.

One of them was Karl Heinz von Oppeln, the son of the governor of Silesia, a state of the old Reich which was annexed by Poland after WWII. His name remains in my memory because, to this day, it is inside an old school atlas that I must have borrowed to copy some maps for an assignment, and which is still in my possession. Based on its size and format, the atlas must have been packed inadvertently among our family albums when we fled from the Soviets in 1945. I learned since then that now the atlas is a collector's item because it contains maps of countries and borders that no longer exist. I also recall the two sons of General Eberhard von Mackensen, Commander-in-Chief of the 1st Panzer Army, a name that is recorded in history of the Eastern front against Stalin and of interest to WWII history buffs. The younger of the two Mackensens, with his tussled blond hair, sat across the aisle from my desk.

Another classmate in Poland was the son of former Field Marshal Walter von Brauchitsch. It was some years ago in New England where my memories were rekindled in a most surprising way, when I again met Hans virtually in my recroom on the Internet, through a German-Language Message Board. He had become a practicing psychiatrist and lived in Chicago. Through the years of our subsequent cyberspace communications, he impressed me as a gentle and brilliant man with incredible insights. Also his wife, Ilse, was an enjoyable computer pal. Sadly, one day in 1998, she informed our internet group that Hans had lost his battle against cancer. Just now, during my moments of recollections about Hans von Brauchitsch, I was motivated to check my computer hard drive, where I had stored some of our discussions. I was pleased to find the following brief excerpts of a 1996 internet conversation, which describes our commiserations of war experiences, as he writes: "Well… on one hand, I AM a shrink. On the other hand, I, too, was expected to be totally in charge of my life since age 12 after I lost my parents. I not only survived, but have always been very proud of the survival skills that I developed during WWII. We Germans are not the only ones who had to grow up in a hurry and still managed to be (because or in spite) quite successful once we become adults. I have seen the same kind of adaptability in, for instance, the children of

Lebanon who, at age 12, were experts in handling a machine gun. They, too, grew up without any visible "trauma" and handled themselves beautifully if and when they became members of adult society. The real victims, unfortunately, were THEIR children. My own girls are now grown up and, thank God, are doing well. But it always was a struggle to me when, as teenagers raised in America's suburbia, they had trouble dealing with such issues as dating, or cheerleading, or not wanting to ride the school bus. After all, when I was their age, I confronted the Commander-General of the French forces to have my visa extended, lived for months on green corn and unripe peaches scrounged from the countryside, survived by trading saccharine and black-market cigarettes for a handful of wheat, etc. There is more than the customary generation gap between those of us who sacrificed our youth to the turbulence of war – and grew by that experience – and of our children of whom we may be subconsciously envious because they were allowed to retain their innocence. Let's hope it works out alright – here, or in Lebanon, or in Serbia... (Signed:) Hans von Brauchitsch."

One more sample of his laconic humor demonstrates my former classmates' disdain for the 12 years of Nazi history when Hans von Brauchitsch posted another note: "You are probably familiar with this anecdote about Hindenburg: After Hitler came to power, the S.A. honored Hindenburg as the titular head of state with a parade. He stood on the balcony, watching the brown-shirts marching, and mumbled: 'Wo kommen denn all die Russen her?' – ('Where do all these Russians come from?')"

In these moments of reflections, I must not overlook one more former classmate of my school years in Poland: Gunther Sachs, of a family whose class of wealthy Germans goes back many generations and, indeed, is among the originators of German industry. His grandfather was the founder of the Opel automobile company. After the war,

Gunther became the first German playboy of international status. His name appears on numerous European tabloids to this day. Beginning in the late 1950s, Gunther was part of what eventually became known as the "Jet Set." His playgrounds were race tracks, Swiss ski resorts, and Monte Carlo, where his tanned face appeared in the company of Prince Renier and Princess Grace of Monaco. He was a regular at the film festivals in Cannes as well as international balls, where he escorted Queen Soraya, then the dismissed consort of the former Shah of Persia. She had taken up residence in Munich. Going for the prize in world glamour, in 1956 Gunther married the French "sex-kitten" Brigitte Bardot in Las Vegas – where they later also divorced. Educated as a mathematician, he wrote a book on Astrology where he formulated some contrived statistics of highly-contested numerical correlations between man and stars. He also dabbled in the production of docu-films and, until recently, he designed calendars and catalogs of beautiful women that drew international photography awards, and which support his charity foundation for neglected children. Today, Gunther ranks among the top five billionaires of Europe.

In the 1960s, while Zach and I lived in Germany, I was once again reminded of my boarding school classmate in Poland, Gunther Sachs, when we bought a Volkswagen as a second car. This specific model was one of the few ever built to operate without a clutch pedal to aid the many postwar amputees in Germany. The clutch was instead activated pneumatically by hand and through an electronic toggle at the end of the stick shift. The patent was called "Saxomat," an innovation by one of Gunther's numerous enterprises.

This "Beetle" was the dealer's only demo at the time, and he was terribly reluctant to let it go. Eventually we brought it to the States, and I am relatively sure that we owned the first 1961 "Automatic Volkswagen" in the USA, because we just never met another VW-owner who was familiar with this kind of automated clutch. In fact, whenever we took the car to a service garage, the mechanic usually scratched his head both in bewilderment – and admiration of our nifty "Saxomat Beetle."

THE WOOD-BURNER

It must have been in 1943 when, one evening after dinner, my father announced that the town of Dolsk had acquired a bus and that, from now on, I no longer needed to commute to school in Srem by horse carriage or sled. The bus had arrived from Germany with its own driver, a former soldier who had lost a leg in the war, and whose name was Joseph. My father explained that, in preparation, the town had built a garage for the bus near the lake, at a section known for its shallow shore where horses were taken to drink and to be washed.

I had never ridden on a bus before and was impatiently waiting for Monday morning to find out what it's like. That's why I got up when the sun began to rise. And instead of waiting for the bus, I grabbed my school bag and hurried to the garage by the lake. And there it was, the bus, in front of the open garage door! I didn't see anyone around until suddenly, as I got closer, I noticed a man in an army uniform on top of the bus. There was a low luggage rack that held a number of burlap sacks, and he was tugging on one of them to drag toward the rear of the bus. When he saw me, he stopped for a moment and, looking down, he shouted, "Gruess di!" I was stunned. That was definitely a "good morning!" in a strong Bavarian dialect. I hadn't heard anyone talk Bavarian since we left Freilassing in 1939 – and now in Poland, this certainly was a happy surprise! I answered, "Are you Joseph?" He seemed pleased that I knew his name and, with "Jawohl. Call me Seppi!" he returned his attention to dragging the burlap sack. When he reached the end of the bus, he opened the sack and, with a clanking racket against the metal, he emptied chunks of wood into a drum which was attached at the middle of the rear bumper and reached to the top of the bus. The "Holzbrenner" (woodburner) resembled an oversized water heater.

Perplexed I asked, "Are you dumping wood into that thing?" He paused and, pressing his thumb against one nostril, blew his nose through the other over the side of the bus. "Without gasoline, I have to fuel it with something," he answered and, looking at his watch, "I'm late, it still needs to be lit." Suddenly, he put his hands on each side of the drum's rim and, with his army boots straight into the air, he made a perfect handstand to peer into its gaping opening. "Just checking" he said laughingly. Astounded, and with great admiration, I told him that I never could stand on my head like that. "That's alright," he said, "I used to be an acrobat." He then took a long metal rod and poked around inside the drum to loosen the woodchips and fill any gaps. Finally he adjusted a small vent on the hinged lid before he dropped it to close the drum. When he climbed down the iron ladder at the side of the bus, one step at the time, it was obvious that he had only one leg, and that he wore a prosthesis. On the ground, while he attempted to ignite the wood, I thought I could hear him utter several hearty Bavarian curses. I watched with fascination the direction of his lighter's flame; it followed a strong draft through the three-inch hole into the base of the drum. Finally, thin white smoke swirled from the vented lid at the top. "Einsteigen!" – ("Get on board!") he ordered with a friendly gesture toward the door.

I was curious to see what the inside of a bus looked like, and eagerly climbed up the steps. Looking around me, I was surprised how roomy it was and how many seats there were, and that they were upholstered in dark blue – and I knew that my school friends, too, would be very pleased.

I chose the seat right behind Seppi's so I could continue to watch him. He first pulled out the choke and, after a few failed cranks, he succeeded to ignite the engine. As the bus began to move, I could smell the faint odor of smoldering wood.

~~~~~~~~~~~~~~~~~~~~~~~~~~~~~

ABOUT PIGEONS AND BAZOOKAS

Years of bombing raids of the Reich had taken its toll and weakened the Wehrmacht along the Russian front due to the lack of supplies. In the late summer of 1944, the German army was in a final retreat. My family, being German civilians in Nazi-occupied Poland, was in grave danger as the Soviets advanced. Radio broadcasts from the front still reported occasional destruction of Russian tanks or hand-to-hand combat when some German unit took out communist partisans in the Carpathian Mountains or in the Balkans. But, generally, these radio messages were the last efforts to under-report the beginning of the end. Stalin's hordes were on their way to overrun Europe.

Since there were no more men of draft-age left, most boys over fourteen at the boarding school in Srem volunteered to join the defense forces. They were assigned a Panzer Faust, the German form of a bazooka, with guidelines how to use it, and then taken in trucks somewhere to the Eastern Front.

A short time later, girls over the age of 14 were also leaving. They were put on a train that took them to the eastern border of Poland where, in preparation of the coming win-

Teenage boys being instructed by a senior citizen, a "Volksturm" man on how to use a "Panzerfaust," a bazooka, to defend Germany against Stalin's Army...

ter, they were to dig trenches ahead of the retreating Wehrmacht. These desperate war efforts left only a few of us ten to thirteen year old children in the classrooms.

That's when, one morning after I arrived at school, I found the teacher leading groups of students to several waiting horse wagons, which took us to a beautiful forest. There we were each given an enamel cup and sent to pick berries. The teacher had brought a large white pail into which we were to empty the berries when our cups were full. She informed us that the berries were going to be made into marmalade for injured soldiers in hospitals. Actually, I was having fun. The sun was shining and the woods in Poland are beautiful, and there were plenty of berries. When nobody was looking, I quickly put a few of the sweet berries in my mouth instead of the cup. This made me feel guilty though, and I did not eat any more berries.

How desperate these last war efforts became can only be measured by what I was to do next – when, one morning, our teacher led us a few blocks from the school to a hospital. There I soon found myself in a dimly-lit cellar next to a pile of dead pigeons. We sat on benches and plucked them. Just like with the berries, we were told that the pigeons, too, were to feed injured soldiers in the hospital. While I plucked them, I did wonder in my twelve year old mind, who had killed so many of them, and how were they killed? The cellar was a dismal place. With all those dead pigeons around us, my classmates and I did not talk much. The pigeons' feathers were of all colors, some were dull gray and others were pure white, so unblemished. As the hours passed, the pile of feathers grew, and I felt sorry for the poor pigeons…

ABOUT BEING ALONE

I was going to be on my own and was determined to be very grown up. I would be alone with only Wanda, the housekeeper, who lived in the kitchen wing of the house. I knew that, for the next few days, nobody would remind me to do my homework or to take a bath, and nobody would tell me what to wear to school. Although Wanda was very pleasant, she spoke little German. I had told my mother that she need not worry about me while she and my father were away.

It was in the fall of 1944, and the Soviets had begun to approach the Eastern border of Poland when a telegram arrived with the message that my brother Ernst, serving as a paratrooper on the Western Front, had been injured. A grenade had exploded near his trench, causing a concussion and bleeding eardrums, and he was in a military hospital somewhere in the Rhineland. My parents left immediately to be with him. He was only seventeen.

Being alone, I began my day very carefully by getting up without delay when I heard the alarm clock. Murrax had been sleeping in my bed, and he seemed reluctant to get out from under the warm featherbed. It was still dark with only the first shimmer of daybreak through the sheer curtains. I could not turn on a light because the town's power station had been shut down for months due to coal shortage, and the only illumination was petroleum lamps. The house was quiet and I shivered in the cold. I hastily gathered a pair of long stockings, a bodice with the garters, my Bleyle slip, a pleated skirt and a sweater – the clothes that I was going to wear to school. On my way toward the stairs, I passed by my parents' open bedroom door; their untouched beds made me feel desolate.

Downstairs, with Murrax trailing behind me, I walked by the dark rooms. I was anxious to get to the living room, where I intended to put on my clothes in front of the stove.

When I opened the door, I was relieved to find Wanda. Seeing her was my reassurance that I was not completely alone
in the big house, alone in all of Poland – in the whole
world! She had just fueled the glazed tile stove with large
chunks of peat. Turning around, she smiled and, with a
strong Polish accent, she said "Guten Morgen, Fraulein." I
was so grateful that I wanted to give her a hug, but I didn't
know Wanda very well.

From the beginning, I noticed that Wanda was a well-
groomed woman who always wore professionally-done hairdos, which she preserved carefully under fine hairnets to
make them last until she had her hair done again. Wanda lit
the ornate petroleum lamp on the dining table, and then
brought a tray with a steaming cup of cocoa and a slice of
bread with butter and jam. As she put my breakfast in front
of me, she pointed at the grandfather clock in the corner of
the room to remind me that I soon will have to get on the
bus that would take me to school in Srem.

That afternoon, when I came home from school, no one
was around. Wagging his tail, only Murrax greeted me in the
living room. After I practiced piano for a while, Wanda
brought my supper and placed it on the dining table. Soon
the room became dark and, knowing that I had lots of
homework to do, I called Wanda to light the lamp on the
table. And then she left the room again. The swinging door
to the kitchen hall closed behind her silently.

I spread several books on the table. My fifth grade geography assignment dealt with colonies and, with the pages of
a large atlas open, I followed the lines that defined the borders of the Belgian Congo on tracing paper. Pouring over
several sources of information, I wrote a report on the
Congo's form of government, the demographic composition, and its agricultural products. As time passed, the silence of the room seemed to penetrate my concentration.
My eyes rose from the paper for a moment and I felt comfort to see Murrax curled up in his basket. Never before had

I heard the clock in the corner tick as loud as it did this evening.

Returning to my tracing paper, I suddenly found a black speck getting in the way of my pen, and I impatiently swept it aside. To my annoyance I noticed that this left a smudge on the paper. Just then another black speck dropped on the paper, and I was puzzled when a whole swarm of black specks dropped on my paper. I finally looked up to find where this unusual shower of soot originated, when my eyes fixed in horror on a tall flame which, like a thin tongue, licked high into the air from inside the cylinder of the petroleum lamp.

I heard myself screaming, screaming, and I seemed to scream without needing a breath, while I sat frozen on my chair. Finally, in the dim end of the room, the swinging door opened a small crack, and one eerily distended and perfectly round eye peeked cautiously through the narrow opening. One more suspenseful moment passed before the door swung open and Wanda entered the room to hastily turn down the wick inside the demonic lamp.

I was still trembling when I went upstairs. Wanda led the way with a candle to light the stairs. At the door to my bedroom she said "Gute Nacht, Fraulein," and I quickly curled up under the safety of my featherbed with Murrax clutched tightly in my arms.

NOSTALGIA ISN'T WHAT IT USED TO BE

Living in Poland during WWII left me with memories of love of the people, a wonderful childhood full of experiences with pets from goats, raccoons, fallow deer, doves, and rabbits – to dogs and horses.

In addition, I was left with the fondness of certain foods that sustained me during those five years of my childhood. Most food items that reached our table came from their di-

My father's love for animals was the motive that he created an amateur zoo in the small park behind the house in Poland. Among raccoons, pheasants, Teal Ducks, peacocks, and a den for Red Foxes, he also kept this pair of Fallow Deer in an enclosure.

rect sources. Our cook bought grain products from a mill somewhere in the area and baked most of our breads and pastry herself. During the war time's food scarcities, producing many acres of sunflowers and harvesting their seeds, we were sent bottles of precious sunflower oil in exchange from a processing company in Germany. And our cook used the oil for rare treats to make wonderful deep-fried foods and desserts.

Milk was brought to the kitchen every morning from the cows or goats in our stables. And I recall curdled milk being drained through a cheesecloth that the cook had tied ingeniously by its four corners to the legs of an upside-down chair with a bowl below inside the inverted seat to catch the whey. With the curds she made several kinds of cheeses. My favorite was a cooked cheese (Kochkaese), which she seasoned with caraway seeds and stirred in a large iron skillet until it turned into glazed bubbles and formed threads. After it cooled, the mass was sliced into wedges like Camembert cheese.

For the greater part of our meat supplies, every year my father brought from Thuringia, Germany, two butchers who stayed for a few days in the guest rooms. Their job was to butcher and process a three hundred pound hog. They used the large kitchen and smoking chamber in the adjoining building to produce the finest variety of smoked sausages and hams. They rendered huge slabs of pork suet to fill earthen jars with lard which we used for cooking and, also, to spread on rye bread with a dash of salt. Following the butchers' work, the odor of spices and smoked meats lingered throughout the house for several days, and their tasty finished products ended up inside a closet made of wooden frames that held tightly woven wire screens; there the smoked hams and sausages were hung to dry. Usually the content of this screen closet supplied our family for a whole year. In addition to poultry, occasionally the cook bought fresh meat from the only butcher in town; and we frequently ate what my father brought home during hunting season, from pheasants and wild boar to deer, as well as twenty-pound hares. A driving-hunt was a method where Polish men

In front of the gate to our house and stables, my father preparing to go on a "drive-hunt" with guests on horse sleds.

My father ready to begin a Drive Hunt at the edge of the frozen lake with group of hunters.

from nearby villages joined in creating a large circle in the open field which they slowly closed, driving rabbits or pheasants into the center, so that the hunters could shoot them.

My mother was an expert in preparing venison. I recall with great fondness the roasted loin of deer when, with a fine knife, she made slits into the lean meat to insert thin strips of salt pork and she created an exquisite sour cream sauce seasoned with bay leaf and capers for the Spaetzle as a side dish.

To add to our diet, my father bought several beehives and a hired man who, wearing a hat from which a veil hung over his face, came periodically to take care of the bees. From the hives, he removed honeycombs that he put inside a centrifuge and, operating a crank, he spun from the combs golden honey, which drained into jars from a spigot. Before each winter, he replaced the honey with sugar syrup inside the hives which he then covered with thick straw mats, to protect them from the cold.

Each fall a great number of hazelnut bushes in the park yielded baskets full of filberts which, to this day, remain my favorite nuts. Raspberries and currants from acres of bushes were taken to processors by truckloads while, for our own use, Wanda – again with the cheesecloth tied to the four legs of an upside-down chair – separated the crushed pulp of berries from the juice to make wonderful jellies, thick bottled fruit syrups as well as currant wine. In fact, two twenty-gallon bottles, nestled in large wicker baskets with glass tubes bubbling from their openings during their fermentation, were left behind standing on the floor of the pantry when we fled from the approaching Soviets. Reflecting on my memories as a refugee, after finding the wine, the Soviets probably had their usual alcoholic rampage when they ransacked through the house upon their arrival in Poland in January 1945.

In my reminiscences I must mention that water in Poland was not potable without being boiled. Typhoid was rampant. Indeed, my brother Ernst and I were struck with the disease the first year we lived in Poland. The illness weakened us to the degree that we literally collapsed and had to be carried from the commode to the bed. While speaking of illnesses, it was many years later in America when my doctor commented, after he scanned my chest x-rays during a bout with pneumonia, that he observed scars on my lungs indicating that, as a child, I must have contracted tuberculosis – which he confirmed with positive skin tests. This finding led me to connect the memory of consuming raw dairy products in Poland, a country which only tested pork for trichinosis in the forties.

The water supply in our household was stored in an attic reservoir, which I never saw. I recall that there was an arm lever in the hall to the kitchen wing, which the maid used several minutes every few days to pump water into the attic tank. The use of the water was limited for washing, for several toilet tanks, and to fill the only water heaters in the house for the two bathrooms that had tubs. Water for drinking had to be boiled daily and stored in the kitchen in an enamel pot with a lid. As a child I disliked the flat taste of boiled, un-refrigerated water – probably the reason that, to this day, I seldom drink water at the table. To deal with the problem, we learned to flavor our boiled drinking water with various fruit syrups, one of which was the bottled currant or raspberry syrups that Wanda made each year. Upon reflection, to this day, I keep bottles of red grape juice in my refrigerator which I mix with water in order to consume the desirable amounts of liquid per day.

Poppy seed, harvested from our fields, was among ordinary staples of our food. Nothing in my memory will surpass the taste of ground poppy seed mixed with raisins and honey that filled the Polish poppy seed cake. Another product of our fields were sugar beets – intended to feed cattle and hogs – however, the cook also boiled them into wonderful brown molasses which was my favorite spread on buttered rye bread.

The most unusual food staple in my childhood probably was smoked eel, which we ate almost every evening for supper. The lake in Dolsk was only a few hundred feet from our entrance-gate and the local fishermen frequently delivered live eel to the kitchen. The eels were as thick as a child's arm and it still gives me shivers when I recall the cook pouring lots of salt into the bucket full of squirming eels to remove their slime so her hands could grab them to cut off their heads and gut them. Afterwards, she strung them on a rod and hung them for several days inside the smoking chamber. After they were smoked and dry, and incredibly aromatic, the eels were served in six-inch segments on individual wooden cutting boards, accompanied by rye bread, butter and radishes or cucumbers.

Last picture in Poland (1943) of my two brothers, before they were drafted into military service. Joachim, my mother, Ernst, I – and Murrax!

CHRISTMAS 1944

Winter spread its cruel season over the battlefields of Eastern Europe. And daily, the radio reported that the German Wehrmacht could no longer hold back the enemy. Stalin's troops had penetrated the eastern border of Poland. Perhaps it was a blessing that, at my age, I did not comprehend the proximity of the Soviets, or its peril.

It was Christmas, and both my brothers were on distant front lines. Ernst was stationed in the west, somewhere near Belgium; and Joachim, according to his last letter, was with a unit in Hungary. Because of uncertainties triggered by the approach of the Russians, his location was of great concern to my parents. At age thirteen, 1944 was to be my most memorable Christmas, as well as our last Christmas in Dolsk.

Snow had fallen all day, and my father sent two horse-sleds to pick up a number of guests from the train station in Srem. They were war-injured officers, among them several amputees. Under a special holiday program related to the circumstances of war, my parents had volunteered to provide a place and environment to celebrate Christmas for injured military men – soldiers who were away from their families, and who were on convalescence leave from the nearby military hospital in Poznan.

In preparation, Mamselle, the cook, had carefully planned the menu. I recall roasted venison and an extravagant dessert – her specialty – consisting of spun sugar that hovered like lace around a golden flan. My mother, with the housekeeper's help, saw to every detail in anticipation of the large number of guests, who also included several families from neighboring estates.

The French doors on the ground floor of the house were opened to enhance the flow between the dining room, my father's library, the drawing room with its magnificent fireplace, and the music salon, where the large Christmas tree created shimmering reflections on the rosewood finish of my mother's Boesendorfer grand piano. The glow from the tree's wax candles lent not only an atmosphere of festivity to the suite of rooms, but also filled the air with gentle pine scent. And, in the hall, the guestbook recorded the arrivals.

I felt uncomfortable standing around. I really wanted to sulk because I had to wear a dark green velvet dress, my first pair of silk stockings – with a garter belt – and black patent shoes that pinched my feet. Being more comfortable in the stable and around my animals, I preferred either boots or sandals. While the house filled with guests, I didn't know what to say each time I was being introduced as the host's daughter. A young officer in jodhpurs – an empty sleeve explained his missing arm – kissed my hand and smartly clicked his heels. In the nick of time, I caught myself from curtseying in response. It was the definitive moment when I realized that I no longer was a little girl.

As the evening passed, the guests wandered through the rooms. Several were on crutches, a few in wheelchairs, and one stood out especially because of the white bandage around his head, implying that he was recovering from a head wound. His appearance reminded me that I had heard my parents or somebody talk about the first pioneering medical procedures of using surgical steel plates in severe war injuries to the head, and I wondered whether, under his bandage, he had such a plate.

During the entire evening, the only conversation I remember as noteworthy was with a soldier in a plain uniform and polished bucket boots. He was there as an aide to one of the officers. He told me that, in civilian life, he actually was an animal trainer and circus acrobat. Right then I admired him and could visualize him climbing among high wires under a striped tent and somersaulting with showmanship onto the backs of trotting horses in a sawdust-covered circus ring.

After dinner, soft piano music broke through the chatter. A Colonel, one leg amputated at the knee, wearing a monocle and his chest ablaze with medals, sat at the piano. Soon men's voices fell into singing Christmas carols. As more injured men gathered around the piano, their voices blended into the familiar melodies of "Oh, Tannenbaum," and "Stille Nacht" – Silent Night...

III.

Crossing the Oder

1945

Refugees' Story of a Trek to
Escape from the Soviets

DAY OF DEPARTURE – JANUARY 21 OF 1945

The anniversary clock took its place among the few personal belongings my mother stowed among feather bedding in one of the boxes. In a similar fashion she packed individually wrapped pieces of a Meissen dinner service. And in another crate, among clothing, she placed several family albums. We were going to travel in a group of three vehicles. In addition to our black carriage, there was a baggage wagon, which, because of its heavy weight, was pulled by a troika, and it was to be last in our small convoy. The vehicle directly behind us was another covered coach, it was to transport a family who the previous summer had been evacuated from Berlin to escape bombing raids. Under a prevailing wartime program they had been assigned spare rooms in our large home in Poland, a country safe from Allied bombs during WWII. These evacuees were a widow and her two little girls. Her husband had been killed on the Western Front. Now they were fleeing again, this time to escape from the advancing Soviets.

The understanding was we would return to the house once the approaching Soviets were driven back and no longer a threat. Despite this hope, my mother took down some of the valuable paintings in case of looting during our absence. She planned to hide them, and for this purpose she asked me to come along to the second floor, so she could show me the secret place she had chosen. There was a door at the end of the hall, which concealed the opening to the flue of a fireplace on the ground floor that was sealed and not in use. Inside the flue, immediately to the left of the door, was a ledge in the wall. That's where she carefully propped three paintings, one of them was a Raphael of the Madonna. Before we went back downstairs, she stopped at the special storage closet to take smoked meats, whole hams and salami sausages. She put them into a burlap sack to take along in the carriage. They were to be our food provisions in case of need.

The house in Dolsk. The entrance to the drive had iron gates; at right is the kitchen wing

By midday the baggage wagon was loaded, which meant we were ready to leave. The widow and her two little girls were already seated inside the brown coach. I grabbed Murrax and, wrapping myself into a blanket, sat next to my mother inside the black carriage. In Poland such carriages were common in the 1940s. They featured leather tops, beautiful facet-cut glass window panes that slid into the door panel when lowered and, inside, tufted velour seats faced each other to accommodate four passengers. The horseman's seat in front was raised and in the open. Wearing mittens, a warm hat and wrapped in fur blankets, he was comfortable even in brutal weather. This type of carriage was fairly heavy and required a sturdy team of horses. Leaving a number of horses behind, my father had selected two of his most prized thoroughbreds to pull the carriage.

Finally our caravan of three vehicles began to move slowly through the gate. January 21 of 1945 was the day we began a trek that was to take us through the perils of the last months of WWII.

We used this type of "Vis-À-Vis" covered carriage to leave Poland.

To leave Dolsk, we needed to pass through the town square. There we found the wagons of hundreds of other German families who had left their homes and belongings. They had already gathered from the 19 surrounding villages that were part of my father's administrative area, the district of Dolsk. Other ethnic Germans who had been traveling through Dolsk for several days from distant places, such as Lithuania and the Ukraine, brought frightening information. They reported the German army was retreating, and the Soviets with their trail of terror were only a few hours to the east. Since most men were away fighting or killed in the war, the majority of refugees were old people, women and children. One could sense among them the dread of the advancing Russians.

Heavy snow began to fall as the refugees were trying to form a convoy. I was astonished when I recognized among them Gerda Matzdorf and Margot Fromm, two women whom my father had hired in the early 1940s, one to manage the kindergarten he had opened in Dolsk, and the other to act as principal of the only German elementary school in the area. Bundled up, the two young women sat on an open cart piled high with their belongings. The cart was pulled by my team of Russian draft ponies, Bobby and Teddy, which my father must have assigned to them, so they too, could escape.

As we approached city hall, I noticed that my father stood in front surrounded by anxious people. Holding a

This two-wheel horse cart was the type Klaus Brobst drove as trek leader

map, he was trying to organize the trek, to explain the projected route that would take them on the road leading westward, and he appointed a trek leader. Klaus Probst, whose young wife and baby were sheltered inside a similar carriage as ours, also traveled among the convoy. A war amputee, he was to take charge. Wearing a fur hat and a bulky lambskin coat, he sat in a two-wheeled gig with his wooden leg propped over a cane. His one-horse vehicle was suitable to make tight turns and ride back and forth and along side the trek to keep the many wagons in line.

Suddenly I became alarmed when I realized that my father might not leave with us – that instead, he was going to stay behind in order to hand the town over to his Polish staff after every German had left Dolsk safely. He appeared by the side of our carriage and, opening the door, he spoke quietly to my mother and then kissed us goodbye. I began to cry – not knowing whether I would ever see my father again…

GROWN UP, SUDDENLY

A mixture of sleet and snow crackled against the carriage windows and, on the icy road, the wheels broke the night air with an eerie ping. To protect my legs from frostbite, my mother kept tucking the fur blanket tightly around my knees. It was only a few weeks ago, and just after I had turned 13, that I had been sick with diphtheria; and she was concerned that I stay warm.

Although it was dark, I knew that since nightfall we had been traveling through the Polish countryside. In many places the shoulder of the road was hidden in deep snow drifts, which called for great skill to guide the horses from getting stuck or the vehicles from turning over. As the hours passed, an ever-growing number of refugees merged into the trek, joining us in the same westward direction.

It had been days since we heard news. In fact, there were no more radio signals, nor were there any newspapers; therefore nobody really knew what was happening. Only word-of-mouth – mostly from fleeing people – described the last days of WWII, the German military collapse on all fronts, and the bombed-out cities. In Eastern Europe, snow-covered roads were crowded mile upon mile with refugees, mostly women and children, terrified of the Soviets' atrocities. Hundreds of thousands had left their homes only hours ahead of Stalin's Red Army, fleeing from his plundering and raping hordes. Some refugees had come from as far away as the Ukraine and Lithuania, others had fled from distant Baltic countries, from East Prussia, Estonia and Latvia. Many had witnessed unspeakable terror, where Stalin's advancing troops had rolled over treks similar to ours, their tanks grinding people and horses into the snow. Survivors who managed to escape were exhausted. They suffered from hunger, and their horses were weakened from the cold weather and days with little rest. Since we had only begun the ordeal a few hours ago, our horses were still able to pass most of their slow and tired treks.

It must have been after midnight when we came abruptly to a halt. With my mittens I scraped crusty frost blossoms from the glass pane to see what was happening outside our carriage. I noticed that we had stopped on a narrow street surrounded by houses. We were in the town of Gostyn, a county seat about 60 kilometers east of the German border, and it appeared the trek had bogged down in a congestion of hundreds of horse-drawn vehicles.

Winter of 1944-45 Treks: *Thousands of refugees fled from Eastern Europe to escape the Soviets.*

Suddenly our carriage door was flung open from the outside and an elderly man, wearing a large fur cap, stood there. I noticed on one sleeve of his thick overcoat he wore an armband, indicating that he was a member of the "Volkssturm." Germans, in their last gasp to form a final defense against Stalin's army, and after no more young men were left, assigned men over sixty to protect women and children from the enemy, often with a hunting rifle or a per-

Soviets machine-gunned and strafed treks, killing civilians and horses.

sonal handgun. It was January 1945, the final days of WWII. "Where is your horseman?" he shouted. "You are blocking the road, we have to move on!" My mother looked startled. "Isn't he on the coachman's seat?" she asked the old man. I unwrapped myself from the blanket to look for Antek. I stepped outside the door onto the running board of the carriage, but his seat was empty with only his blanket draped over it. The reins were neatly wrapped around the brake handle. Alarmed, I jumped down on the snow-packed road to check our other two vehicles behind us and to my shock, I found that their horsemen too, were gone. Considering the most recent developments of the war, it was not surprising they had left us. After all, they were Poles who, while taking us to safety, had left their own families behind; and, in view of the approaching Soviets, they had no reason to feel that they were still employed by us fleeing Germans. It was understandable they chose to make their way back to Dolsk while no one saw them leave in the dark.

After taking note of our predicament, the old man with his Volkssturm armband turned to me. "You need to take over one of your vehicles, I'll see if I can find some more able-bodied people to drive your other wagons. We have to move on!" With that he disappeared into the dark to search the trek for another old man with an armband. My mother was upset, and we both realized that she would be of no help. I quickly took a blanket from the carriage and wrapped it around my head and shoulder to protect myself from the wind-driven snow, and standing in the road, I waited. The old man came back, and with his steaming breath, shouted he had found somebody to drive the baggage car at the rear. He told me to take the reins of the coach with the Berliner widow, and he proceeded to climb on the empty seat of the black carriage, ready to lead the way.

Not wasting any time, I ran back to the other carriage where the Berliner mother stood in the road crying, "How are we going to continue without a horseman?" I quickly informed her of what had happened, and that I was going to drive the team. With great alarm I noticed that the old man had begun to move the black carriage ahead, and I yelled at the widow to return to her seat, that we must hurry. I was terrified I might get separated from the Volkssturm man ahead of me with my mother inside the carriage. Losing them in the dark was a dangerous possibility, as had often happened to many refugees among the miles of treks when others, cutting in between vehicles, caused family members to never see one another again. I hastily climbed on the seat, wrapped the blanket tightly around my knees, grabbed the reins and whip, and hissing through my teeth to signal the team to pull forward, I quickly closed the gap between me and my mother's carriage – as we moved into the night…

CROSSING THE ODER

The snow stopped, but the cold wind prevailed. We traveled a few more hours and the horses began to tire. Klaus Probst, in his gig, pulled up alongside the carriage to pass the word that we would stop for the night in the next village. Later, he directed us into a farm yard. There, one of the old Volkssturm men and I unhitched the seven horses and watered and fed them. Before going to sleep in the hayloft above the stable, my mother and I ate some bread with slices of smoked salami from the burlap sack. Uniquely comforting are memories of not being hungry, when having little food.

Next day, we continued our trek. Traveling over 30 kilometers per day we reached the river in Guben, south of Frankfurt on the Oder. It was getting dark and, approaching the bridge, the trek of hundreds of refugees came to a slow halt. Sleet had fallen on the steaming backs of the weary horses. Holding the reins for hours, my hands had become numb. The damp blanket around my knees felt heavy and no longer warm, and I feared that the stinging pain in my calves was from the onset of frostbite. Up ahead, I heard voices shouting – then Klaus, the trek-leader, appeared to inform the drivers that the bridge across the river had been destroyed by bombs and that German troops were in the process of laying pontoons. As soon as they were in place, we would be able to cross the river and continue our flight from the advancing Soviets.

It had been days since we left Poland during the night of the blizzard and now, when we finally had reached Guben, we were not able to cross the river. The Oder had been our goal as well as of countless other refugees who sought safety on the west bank of the river from Stalin, whose murderous troops were coming closer every day.

Since we began the flight, I had lost all perception of time. Conventional sources of news no longer existed. At the beginning of the ordeal, only fragmented information reached us from the collapsing Eastern Front when the Wehrmacht were no longer able to hold the Soviets back. Only through reports passed among the refugees did we learn of the massacres of entire villages and the tragedy in East Prussia, where advancing Soviets mangled thousands of fleeing women and children under their tanks, deliberately rolling over their treks on the road. Others described when Stalin's hordes gang-raped women in Latvian villages, and that thousands of people were deported to Siberian forced-labor gulags. Every day brought terrifying accounts from those who had escaped. Already weeks before our own departure from Poland, thousands of refugees from Lithuania and Latvia had arrived in our town near Poznan. They were among the first of millions of refugees who would continue to leave their distant parts of Eastern Europe, a flood of pitiful humanity trying to escape Stalin's atrocities. As night settled over the banks of the river, an ominous sense of danger spread among us. I covered the tired horses with blankets and, trying to warm up, I cowered next to my mother in the rear of the carriage and waited.

A deep red horizon signaled daybreak when I heard men's voices, "The pontoons are in place, we can cross the river!" I hastily removed the blankets from the horses. The sound of gravel under the wheels told me that the trek in front was beginning to move. Because the bridge lay in rubble, we had to leave the road to approach the river's edge. I used all my strength of a thirteen year old to pull the brakes so not to lose control of the wagon on the steep bank. After I managed to bring the horses' straining efforts into balance with the weight of the wagon, we slowly moved forward on the slippery, sleet-covered grass and rocks. Walking along the side of the team, I was anxious to keep a safe distance from the wagon in front, or else the shaft might ram its back. Finally the hollow sound of the floating pontoons under the pounding hooves gave the welcome signal of gaining distance from the advancing Soviets.

~~~~~~~~~~~~~~~~~~~~~~~~~~

THE REFUGEE CAMP

When we reached the other side of the Oder, our trek had traveled approximately 150 kilometers. Just before moving on, my father appeared suddenly at the side of our carriage. It had been days since we left Dolsk, and he had finally caught up with us. While on the road, I didn't realized just how much I had suppressed my anxiety, agonizing whether he would escape before the Soviets reached Dolsk, and whether he was alive. I scrambled off the carriage seat to hug him. Relieved to see him, I was near crying. When he noticed that I had been driving the team, he was upset, yet he was not surprised that our horsemen had deserted us. He explained that he left Poland in the town's small fire truck only a few hours before the Soviets arrived. To deal with the difficulty of thousands of refugees who

Typical refugee camp in 1945 (left). Horse trek in the winter of 1945.
Thousands of refugees on the roads fleeing from the Soviets (right).

continued to flee across the Oder-Neisse, he was now under
orders by the Reich's agency for refugees, to set up a camp
in Jueterbog, in a large state forest south of Berlin. For this
reason, he had to leave us again. Before he returned to his
truck, he promised to meet us in Falkenberg as soon as he
could.

After having crossed the Oder at Guben, our trek of
hundreds of vehicles, was now disbanding. To follow my
father, the majority of wagons turned northwest toward
Jueterbog. The widow and her two little girls, however,
joined another group of refugees; they continued their trek
into the opposite direction, toward Dresden. These developments left only us, the carriage and baggage wagon,
driven by the elderly Volkssturm man, to travel to Falkenberg on the river Elster.

~~~~~~~~~~~~~~~~~~~~~~~~~~~~~

MY FATHER AND FALKENBERG

Falkenberg was my father's hometown. That's where he
owned an apartment house on Friedrich Strasse, the
main street, as well as a single house on the outskirts. Falkenberg is the town my parents began their married life after my mother left Munich, and where all three of us chil-

dren were born. Also living in Falkenberg were my beloved Elsa Born and her parents, "Tante Martha and Papa." The cemetery with graves of my father's family was also located in Falkenberg, and in 1918, after WWI, he returned to Falkenberg from the front in the Crimean.

Just as we were ready to turn toward Falkenberg, we learned that Klaus Probst, our trek leader, had lost the horse that pulled his gig. Actually, from the time we left Dolsk and before he shot the horse, I had noticed that it was nearly without fur, a sign of demodectic mange, a condition that can infect entire stables. Indeed, the team that pulled his wife's carriage showed the same symptoms. Without hair, the horses' skin appeared pale red. To protect them from the harsh weather, they were covered with blankets. In all likelihood, the carriage horses too, would need to be destroyed soon.

Klaus' wife, Brigitte came to speak to my mother. She was a pretty woman, petite and with an unusual hairdo, a single blonde braid wrapped around the crown of her head. Holding her baby in her arm, I noticed that she was near tears and very troubled. Klaus could no longer find stables that would allow his weakened animals to stay, for fear that they might spread the mange. At the moment he was negotiating with somebody to leave them behind. My mother put her arm around the young woman and helped stow her few belongings into our carriage. This meant they would travel with us to Falkenberg. Instead of me driving our team again, Klaus now took the reins and I joined the two women in the carriage. The baby girl's nose was running, a sign that she had a cold, and her cheeks looked bright red from fever. To feed the infant, I was touched when Brigitte put the baby's bottle between her bare thighs to warm the cold milk.

Mindful to avoid potential targets of bombing raids, we traveled on country roads and by-passed Cottbus, a major industrial city. Trekking through the open country side, occasionally we noticed high in the sky large formations of bombers, sometimes accompanied by the white puffs of German flak. Today I know these planes were American Flying Fortresses or British Lancasters on bombing missions over Berlin, Stettin, Hamburg, or any of the 120 cities that were turned to rubble and, which by the end of the war, had killed over 900,000 German civilians.

At nightfall we arrived in Elsterwerda, a small town approximately 50 kilometers north of Dresden, and we stabled the horses on a farm. We were tired and, just as we prepared to find a place in the barn to sleep, my mother called my attention to look south into the distance. The dark sky accentuated the horizon which pulsated in eerie orange

Dresden February 13-14, 1945:
I have not seen a recent study on the still widely-ignored Forced Exodus of Germans from East Europe, but am familiar with Markusen and Kopf, The Holocaust and Strategic Bombing: Genocide and Total War in the 20th Century, 1995, which classified the strategic bombing offensive against Germany as genocidal.

flashes. We watched in awe. The air throbbed with percussive waves that seemed to reach inside my chest. It was the night of February 13-14, 1945, the Fire-Bombing of Dresden…

The next morning I woke to the sound of voices, the chatter of women. After a moment I realized that their language was not German. Rising from the warm straw, I hastily brushed off my clothes and my hair, and when I walked toward the barn door to investigate where the voices came from, I met my mother coming toward me from the farmyard. She had already been awake to use the farmer's outhouse and, leaning forward, she whispered. "Be careful when you go outside! A group of women prisoners must have stayed overnight in the shed next to the barn." She added that a few old men in tattered Wehrmacht uniforms were guarding them, and that one of the men had told her that they were under orders to take the women to the west, to escape from the advancing Soviets. My mother elaborated that he and his two fellow guards were terrified of what will happen to them, once the group reaches the Allied Forces. The guards feared that they either would be shot, or beaten to death by their prisoners.

As I stepped out from under the barn door, I noticed about sixty women in various stages of undress in front of the adjacent shed. Evidently, using the warm rays of the sun, they were washing themselves and their striped prison garb. Some helped each other shampoo their hair. The warm water they used came from the large "Gulaschkanone," the German term for a military field kitchen. Typically mounted on two wheels, a Wehrmacht "goulash cannon" was a large kettle on top of a fire box from which emerged a tall stove pipe. The cart was usually pulled behind a truck or by horses in military convoys. But in this case, in order to prepare their food along the way, the women must have pushed the goulash cannon themselves from the time they were evacuated from a camp.

I had never seen camp inmates before and, for a while, I watched the group. With rifles hanging loosely from their shoulders, the elderly men seemed uncomfortable having to guard the women in their intimate activities. I felt sorry for them all.

Years later, as the story of the holocaust unfolded, I remembered this incident. And I wonder to this day, why, instead of being killed, these inmates were evacuated from a death camp – or why their German guards did not shoot them – even just to save themselves. I pray that the guards eventually abandoned their prisoners in time, so that they all survived the last days of the war...

After another day on the road, our small caravan arrived in the town of my birth, Falkenberg on the Elster. The Soviets had not yet crossed the German border from Poland, and we felt safe for the moment.

Klaus Probst, his wife and baby found shelter in the home of a friend's of my parents near the center of town. Under the catastrophic conditions, and thanks to their kindness, we were able to stay at the home of Elsa's parents. We stored the crates of the baggage wagon in their basement. As to the horses, one team was stabled in a nearby country estate, and the other with a large bakery.

Driving his small fire truck into the yard, my father arrived a few days later. He had come from the refugee camp in Jueterbog, about 30 kilometers north of Falkenberg.

When he had first caught up with us in Guben, we did not realize that, in his truck, he had brought with him a Short-Haired Pointer puppy – the new hunting dog he had just bought before the Soviets advanced into Poland. He evidently had not been able to leave the puppy behind.

Now, adding to our calamities, we also had to take care of little "Faust," the poor puppy who was only about four months old. His ribs showed under his loose skin – obviously he was famished. Considering our own shortages, it became a daily challenge to find food for him. We managed to fill buckets with diluted leftovers, chicken entrails stretched with bread, potatoes or bran, and occasionally mixed with milk. He slurped up this swill with gusto, distending his poor belly at least for a few hours.

Because there was ample room on the truck, my father also brought a rolled-up oriental rug from the house. And among the final items, bizarre as any cargo can be, was a carton that contained a life-size bust of Hitler wrapped in a Nazi flag. These things had been part of the furnishings in his office at city hall in Dolsk. Naturally, before he turned over the office to the Polish city council, he removed the objects. Now we had to dispose of the cursed stuff. But where – and without delay?

A MACABRE FUNERAL

Elsa's house was located on the outskirts of Falkenberg in the shadow of a towering wind mill on the narrow country lane. Along its edge and across from the house was the low brick wall of an ancient cemetery. Being the youngest of twelve children, the cemetery held the graves of my father's parents and several of his six brothers. In the evening, just as it began to get dark, I remember that I accompanied him to the graveyard. He carried a spade and the carton with Hitler's life-size bust and the flag. After he found his brother's grave and, after clearing groundcover and dry leaves, he dug about two feet deep into the mound and placed the contents of the carton into the hole. He covered it with soil and replaced the ivy ground cover and loose leaves.

BOMBS AND DOGFIGHTS

To contribute scarce food during our stay at Elsa's house, my mother set out early one morning to walk about five kilometers into town in order to register our family at the office for ration cards in Falkenberg's city hall. She was gone for about an hour and I was standing in the yard when I heard the droning approach of a formation of bombers. In awe, I observed strings of black pearls tumbling from below their bellies. As the bombs glided right above my head in a diagonal direction toward Falkenberg, they emitted the sound of an organ's bass pedals that are pushed down all at the same time.

Oh my God! Watching their course, I realized that the bombs would hit the area where my mother was. With horror, I noticed their impact. Within seconds, a progression of black plumes of smoke – one following the other – rose at the horizon. After several moments, the delayed sound waves filled the air with a rumbling roar.

As soon as the planes disappeared, I ran and kept running – and running – to find my mother. I followed the black smoke in the distance, which led me to the railroad station. Running through the empty streets I was terrified – there were no people.

Suddenly, air raid sirens wailed into my ears. Was there to be another bombing raid? Instinctively I looked for cover and found myself in front of a large brick building. The wide steps toward the entrance looked like those of a school or an office building. Mounted on its side, I recognized a large sign that suggested a public air raid shelter. I ran up about six steps and reached the recessed entrance. I tried to open the door but, like in a nightmare, the door was locked.

Just then, a woman and a little boy, wearing a Hitler Youth uniform, rushed up the stairs. She too, seemed to have followed the sign to the public air raid shelter and she joggled the handle of the locked door as well, with no avail.

Suddenly, low-flying fighter planes – accompanied by the clatter of machine guns – took over the sky. Between the air above me and the railroad station across the street, the small agile planes performed the perplexing maneuvers of a dogfight.

Huddling next to the woman and her child, I pressed my body against the door inside the recess. After a while, and without reason, the erratic planes, the racket of their guns, and their tumbling acrobatics, vanished. A deadly silence followed the fracas and generated my urge to run away, to flee from under the recess. As my foot stepped forward, I felt a hand push me back against the door.

That's when the deferred deluge of shrapnel began to fall from the sky. Thousands of hissing, red-hot chunks of metal hit the steps right in front of me, each releasing a thin trail of smoke.

When the deadly shower ceased, I finally ran from under the recess. I looked back for the woman with the little Hitler Youth boy, but there was nobody there…

Later that afternoon, my mother returned from Falkenberg. Her hair and clothing were covered with dust. She had survived the bombing raid inside a basement of an apartment house that was damaged and where the cellar door had collapsed under the pressure of the explosions. She described the hysteria that broke out inside the crowded shelter, and how several injured people were pulled from the debris.

It took several days before my mother recovered from the terror.

Falkenberg Railroad station 1935, before bombardment 1945.

My Comment:

Naturally, after the many years, I can not recall the date when Falkenberg was bombed. The access to sources of recorded history on the Internet are incredible, because I just now searched for the date of bombardment of Falkenberg, and found this diary by a US Air Force Officer:

Welcome to the official 381st Bomb Group (Heavy)

Memorial Association & Triangle-L Society web site, commemorating the service of all USAAF units assigned to Station 167 – Ridgewell, England, during World War II. 532nd Bomb. Sq., 381st Bomb Group (H) - WAR DIARY Submitted by 1st Lt William E. Kornermann

APRIL 1945

17. Today our ships went to Dresden to attack the locomotive repair depot, which was bombed visually but wet prints show the results as poor. Air opposition was nil and flak meagre and inaccurate. Lts Kreamer and Bailey led the high squadron, with: Lts Huff, McDonald, Hendricks, Instone, Baker, Firlit, Van Steenkist, and Castille.

18. Non Operational. The following enlisted men were trans-ferred to the infantry today: Cpl Witt, Pfc Frost, Pfc Girdano, Pvt Stansbury and Pvt Knight.

19. Our target for today was the railroad bridge at Elsterwerda 16 miles west of Ruhrland, and important link in the east-west German supply lines. Our squadron which led the group, did not bomb the #1 target, but **hit the rail centre at Falkenberg** visually with good results. No enemy opposition was encountered and flak was meagre and inaccurate in the Ruhrland area. Lt Seeley led the group with Lt Bailey, the other pilots being: Lts Baker, Castille, Van Steenkist, Instone, Firlit, Poland, McDonald and Sikes. Etc…

ERNST !

I can't recall the moment when it happened or how my brother Ernst appeared.

After we had stayed at Elsa's house for several weeks, there he was one day, dragging a burlap sack. He was dirty and his face was covered with stubble, a sign he must have been on the road for days. He was thin and wore the tops of striped hospital pajamas, a pair of grimy uniform pants, and his bare feet were swimming inside boots far too large for him. And, I

My brother, Ernst Wolfgang Koppe, born: April 1, 1926.

can't forget that Ernst was infested with lice. My mother led him behind hedges into a private corner of the yard, where she took off his clothes so that they could be burned later. Elsa's Papa provided my mother with a jar of petroleum, which somehow was used to exterminate Ernst's body vermin.

He had just turned eighteen, and it was a miracle that he had found us and that he was alive! Ernst, having pursued his hobby and training as a glider pilot from the age of fourteen and, after he was drafted at the age of seventeen, had become a paratrooper in the German military.

Last we knew was that he was recovering from an injury in a "Lazarett," a military hospital, in the Rhineland. His last Feldpost letter (APO mail), had arrived in Poland weeks before Christmas of 1944. Since the collapse of the Western Front, we were forced to assume that he was missing in action.

As it turned out, he had been transferred to a military hospital in Berlin. When he heard rumors that the hospital (and Berlin) was to be turned over to the approaching Soviets, he and another injured "Kumpel" (fellow GI) escaped through a window. From there, Ernst walked several days to Falkenberg, a distance of eighty miles.

He had no way of knowing whether we would be there, whether we had fled from Poland, or even had escaped from the Soviets! Considering our past family connections with Falkenberg, however, he could think of no better place to go. That he found us there at Elsa's house, was again one of the amazing twists of divine providence that followed each of us during our travails.

The only possession Ernst had with him was in this sack. It was filled with large, jagged slabs of chocolate. On their way, he and his pal had run across a bombed-out factory. There they found man-sized vats lined with chocolate which they chiseled off with a screw driver.

〰〰〰〰〰〰〰〰〰〰

LEAVING FALKENBERG

As long as we had stayed at Elsa's house in Falkenberg, my father was still under assignment by the government's "Refugee Office" to assist the people who had fled from Dolsk and its district. Their horse treks were stranded, along with thousands of others, in the camp in Jueterbog.

Of course, he no longer had any gas to drive the small fire truck, and I rode with him on one of his trips to the camp in a horse-drawn wagon. Trotting for hours on a monotonous country road, the front edge of one of the tired horses' hooves wore off – right through the iron of the shoe. Having traveled 30 kilometers north of Falkenberg, we passed through a large state forest as we approached the camp.

I suddenly could smell cadaver. My father explained that, due to the shortage of fodder, the refugees' horses were dying in masses, that there were not enough able-bodied people to bury them fast enough, and that there was no fuel to burn them.

By then, my father must have decided that with the continuing approach of the Soviets, we would soon leave Falkenberg to resume our trek westward. Returning from his final trip to Jueterbog, he brought a fresh team of black horses, which would have faced the same fate of starvation, had he left them at the camp.

Accompanying this handsome team was their Polish horseman by the name of Josef. He wanted to leave the camp too, and joined my father. This last trip from Jueterbog proved to be a perilous experience for them. Fighter planes deliberately strafed the road. My father described how he stood outside on the running board of the carriage looking for the planes, so that Josef could quickly drive under trees seeking camouflage.

The day Stalin's invasion troops broke through the German border in the East, we left Falkenberg and Elsa's house, to resume our trek. The date must have been around the twentieth of April.

We were relieved that this time Ernst was with us, but also deeply concerned about Joachim's whereabouts. His last Feldpost letter had come from Hungary, several months ago.

The next river we had to cross this time was the Elbe. On the way, by nightfall we anticipated to pass through Muehlberg, where we planned to stay overnight at the estate of close family friends. Their name was Friese. I remember them as being my godparents. After several hours on the road, Josef drove the carriage through the gate of the estate. As we came near the house, we were struck with horror to find the couple dead, hanging from the balcony of the second floor. The sight was so grisly that, without stopping, we turned around in revulsion and fled. Apparently, as the Soviets approached, the Polish workers on their farm had killed them.

My Comment:

When my father returned from the First World War, he found his country taken over by Anarchists and Bolsheviks. And the Allies had saddled Germany with The Peace Treaty of Versailles.

At the end of WWI, Germany had lost control of important industrial areas, was burdened with the Versailles Treaty, reparations, and experienced an inflation rate that could raise the price of a loaf of bread from 1 billion Marks in the morning to 20 billion Marks at night. These were the combined reasons that my father became involved in politics, and in 1928 he was elected to the House of Representatives of the State of Saxony during the Weimar Republic. With the struggle for political control, the country continued to suffer from dissolution, and cities experienced street battles between radical factions. Under the reverberations of the 1917 Bolshevik revolution in Russia, Communist expansionism, and the destruction of European monarchies; Communists emerged as the most powerful

My father, Adolf Robert Koppe, 1893-1958, WWI member of the Kaiser's Heavy Cavalry – Master of Music Corps, Munich, where he later met my mother. Elected in 1928 to the House of Representatives, State of Saxony, Weimar Republic. In this picture, the Iron Cross, the ribbon in the button hole, indicates he had been in WWI combat in the Crimean.

political opposition in Germany. My father opted to join the only party that opposed Communism. This choice led to his affiliation with the "Stahlhelm" – (Steel Helmet,) a patriotic movement whose membership consisted mostly of WWI veterans. They represented the only viable resistance

*to the Communist party, which in Germany was led by
Reds like Karl Liebknecht and Rosa Luxemburg, foreigners
who had appointed themselves as "Citizens of the Proletar-
iat..." In due course, my father's political resistance to
communism resulted in his appointment to his civil service
office after the Nazis defeated the communists in 1933.*

*Adolf Robert Koppe, elected 1928 to the House of Representatives, State
of Saxony Weimar Republic (left). After the defeat of Communism in
1933 being escorted by his constituents in Falkenberg (right).*

*My Father's
birthplace with
mounted
commemorative
plaque in
Prestewitz,
Sachsen Anhalt
(Saxony).*

EUROPE AFTER WORLD WAR ONE

The map above shows the Germans' courageous resistance against Soviet ambitions of expansionism into all of Europe after WWI. Notwithstanding Hitler's infamous legacy, historically the Nazi movement became the only opposition against communism in Europe. Soviet expansionism, beginning after WWI, helps explain why Hitler eventually came to power in Germany.

IV.

Crossing the Elbe

1945

The Story of a Trek to Escape from the Soviets

OSCHATZ

On April 25, 1945, we crossed the Elbe in Strehla, the same day that Soviets and American combat troops met in Torgau at the banks of the Elbe, 10 km to the north. At last, we crossed the historic river. Glancing back once more, seared into my memory to this day remains a bizarre sight: silhouetted against the rising sun above the eastern bank of the Elbe was one of the last German heavy infantry cannons in retreat – pulled by oxen...

Only years later, after dates and events fell into place, were we able to appreciate the amazing chance to have crossed the Elbe just hours before the Soviets arrived. Torgau was to become a historical landmark. Soviet and American veterans would travel there, even during the Cold War (!), to celebrate the anniversaries of victory over Nazi Germany and the alliance between Roosevelt and Stalin. Standing at the banks of the Elbe, communist Russians and American veterans shook hands, and posed before the media.

As soon as the road was wide enough, Josef steered the team to the side of the road and stopped for a moment so that Ernst could get out of the carriage. Despite the miserable circumstances, I had to suppress laughing out loud when I looked at the fringed babushka that covered his head. His face was deliberately smudged with dust. He immediately began to remove his disguise as an old woman and loosened the belt which he had used to tuck a blanket around his waist, creating a skirt. He had worn this zany

American and Soviet troops shake hands on a "Bailey Bridge" over the Elbe River in April 25, 1945.

get-up in case the Soviets caught up with us and searched the dark inside of the carriage. Stalin's troops were under orders to shoot on sight any young German male, especially if he was taller than six feet, in their assumption that he was a member of the Waffen SS.

By midday we entered Oschatz, which by then was occupied by Americans. After weeks on the road, we were relieved to have reached safety from the Soviets at last! Thousands of refugees milled trough the small town on its main road. Many of them pulled carts, pushed baby carriages or bicycles, loaded with their few belongings. Others moved along in slow horse-drawn vehicles like ours. In addition to the refugees, loose formations of men in tattered uniforms, noticeably representing various nationalities, trod along the dusty road. They appeared to be released prisoners of war from stalags. To my astonishment, I noticed that there were also a number of men who walked into the opposite direction, back toward the Elbe, from where we had just come. This implied that they were East Europeans released from German POW camps, released communist prisoners from Russia, Poland, Rumania and – who knows – what Soviet Satellite country they intended to return to. Another group's striped prison suits suggested that they were liberated concentration camp detainees. The most startling sight was a large number of young men uniformly dressed in white tee shirts emblazoned with black swastikas across the chest. In need to replace their prison garbs, they must have looted a German military supply depot somewhere along the way.

Josef drove the team slowly through the crowd. Our black leather carriage stood out in an ostentatious way among most refugees' potato wagons, some pulled by oxen or bony dairy cows. At this point, anything with wheels was part of the wretched scene.

It was in Oschatz, where we encountered the first American tanks and military vehicles, among them olive colored trucks with the white star painted on the doors. They were loaded with American troops. And I also saw, for the first time, an American Jeep. I was puzzled by a tall iron pole mounted vertically on the center of the jeep's front bumper. Later, I found out that the pole was to break wires stretched across the road by potentially hostile Germans, intended to decapitate the American driver. In retrospect, I never saw such wires, nor heard of any decapitations.

April was the month when we believed to finally have reached safety since we left Poland in January; and it was the month of Ernst's birthday. He had just turned eighteen. Yes, April the First is his birthday. And we had fooled the Soviets…

There was no way of telling whether, by traveling to the next town, we would encounter fewer refugees with their carts or thousands of released prisoners. For this reason, we hoped that we would find among the farms along the road one that had room in a barn for the horses and shelter for us, as well. When my father saw an open gate, he ordered Josef to quickly steer the carriage into the yard. I watched my father talk to the farmer, who had come out of the barn. After a few moments, I was thankful when my father signaled that we could stay. Josef unhitched the horses and led them to the trough to drink, and then into the stable to be fed and to rest. Since the farmer had already taken in other refugees, he had no more room for us in the house, but he sent my mother and me across the street, where an elderly couple had a small room on the second floor of their house. Ernst, my father and Josef were glad to sleep in the hayloft above the stable.

For the remainder of the day, thousands of displaced victims of war continued to mill through the street. As a sign that we were safe from the Soviets, we were relieved to see on the street also the presence of American occupation forces. For a moment, my attention was drawn to a couple of GIs who had jumped off the back of their truck and, holding a rifle, one knelt in front of a road sign that read "180 km to Berlin," while the other took pictures. They may not have known, but their snapshots recorded a significant moment of history that nobody could yet comprehend fully...

Every resident and home owner along the street was vulnerable to the masses of tired foreigners and desperate refugees who continued to crowd the small town. Later that afternoon I was astonished when, across the street from the stables, I saw my father sitting on a chair in front of the house where my mother and I were to stay for the night. At his feet was a bucket, and as people walked by, he offered them water to drink from an enamel cup. I was baffled by his action. I didn't understand why he would make contact in this manner with strangers. He could barely keep up with passing cup after cup of water to eager hands. He finally had a short break to answer my question, "When I offer people water, they keep moving on instead of trying to get into the house," he explained. The elderly owners of the house were thankful to my father for this novel effort.

Suddenly, the sound of blaring loudspeakers from a slowly-moving American Jeep announced in German a military order that, under threat of severe penalty, civilians must turn in all guns and radios to a certain designated area in town by the next morning. We did not have weapons and no longer had a radio. Actually, nobody had heard any German language radio signals in days. As the Jeep drove back and forth, its loudspeakers kept repeating the same message the rest of the afternoon.

By evening, my mother prepared some food for us in the farmer's kitchen. As so many times during our flight, she fried in a skillet several slices of salami from the sack of smoked meats that had sustained us since we left Poland in January. The farmer's wife gave us a few potatoes,

In 1945, with the collapse of the German defense against Stalin,
millions of German refugees fled to escape from the advancing Soviets.
At right, German homeless families trekking through Berlin.
(Army Photograph)

which made the meal better than we had had in a long
time. There, in the kitchen I met Erika, a pretty blonde
girl in her early twenties. She and her parents were
among the refugees who had also found shelter in the
farm the day before we arrived. To flee from the Soviets,
they had left East Prussia by horse trek, similar to our
circumstances.

〰〰〰〰〰〰〰〰〰〰〰〰

DAY OF INFAMY

The next morning, standing at the gate of the farm, I
watched the continuous traffic of refugees with their
carts, wagons pulled by horses or oxen, and processions of
released POWs of numerous nationalities. The street was lit-

American troops arrive at the Elbe, before withdrawing with the arrival
of the Soviets (left). Refugee Treks filling miles of roads of East Europe,
with the advance of the Soviets (right).

Millions of expelled ethnic Germans from East Europe trekked through Germany. Absorbing them in bombed and war-ravaged West Germany created enormous difficulties of famine and homelessness.

tered with horse apples, loose wheels, broken-down carts, rags and pieces of discarded uniforms.

That's when my attention was drawn to a horse without a harness that stood there by the curb, its head hung low dejectedly. I found it odd, considering that all draft animals were in great demand. Perhaps it was sick. In the assumption that the poor animal was thirsty, I followed my impulse and rushed to take it by the halter and lead it into the yard, to the trough to let it drink. It seemed forever before his head came back up with a loud snort. I didn't know what else to do, so I just left it standing there.

Suddenly, the massive droning sound of engines penetrated the air. American tanks, Jeeps and trucks, filled with troops, nearly forced the crowds of refugees and POWs off the street. I was puzzled. Why were Americans now moving westward, away from the Elbe? Were they retreating from the approaching Soviets? That's when I saw an American POW break away from a group of pedestrians to run after one of the trucks. Doing so, he dropped the handle of the small cart that contained his possessions and he shouted, "Hey Joe! Wait for me!" Several hands reached down to pull him into the moving truck. Having observed the American find a ride, I dodged the crowds to quickly secure his discarded handcart. I pulled it into the yard and determined right then to claim it as mine. I examined its content, which consisted of the first American things I had ever seen. There was an ugly olive green army t-shirt, a pair of army boots, a toilet case, a mess kit, and a small packet with the letters that spelled Wrigley's Spearmint Gum. I had never seen chewing gum before, and didn't know what to do with, so I tossed it aside. What mainly triggered my fascination was a paperback book with dog-eared pages. Paperbacks are an American invention. Being curious, I leafed through it to test my school-English, whether I could actually read a book in the English language. Later I showed it to the young boy who, with his mother, lived across the hall upstairs in the same house where we had found shelter. Egmar right away ran to get his pocket-size German-English dictionary. We both sat down on the bench by the stables and tried to read the book.

Little did I know that this was the day when American troops began their withdrawal in preparation of not just turning the entire state of Saxony, or half of Germany over to Stalin, but also half of Europe; ten nations – one hundred million people – were to be handed over to Stalin by the Western Allies, abandoned into the brutal gulag system and terror of the Soviets.

TRUMAN LIBRARY PICTURES

Title: "American and Russian soldiers dancing after a dinner." Date: April 27, 1945

Americans and a Soviet woman, celebrating.

Mongolian Troops – WWII American Allies – Soviets in Germany

*Title: Churchill, Stalin, and Truman shaking hands at the Potsdam
Conference, discussed post-war arrangements in Europe, July 23, 1945.
Pictured: Churchill, Winston, Sir, 1874-1965; S; Stalin, Joseph, 1879-
1953; Truman, Harry S., 1884-1972*

*Document File Photograph by the US Army, 1945
German rape victim.*

Translation: *"Children were forced to watch their mothers being raped and murdered. Many women became pregnant,
many contracted VD. They had no hope that somebody would
come to their aid. In order to escape the violence, and from
falling repeatedly into the hands of their abusers, they hid in
forests, attics and cellars. The trauma they suffered continues
to torment their lives. 'In quiet moments, at night when it is
quiet, before I go to bed, after I said my prayer and I am all
alone, I am overcome,' confesses Christel Jolitz, whose tragic
fate can not be put into words." (End of translation.)*

"Rape and Murder" Film document of the US Army:

Vergewaltigung und Mord

Filmdokument der US-Army,
Tschechoslowakei 1945.

"Wer das Schwert nimmt, der wird durchs Schwert umkommen. Für was sollten wir noch Gefühle haben? Die Deutschen haben uns zuerst angegriffen," schildert der russische Frontkameramann Aleksej Semin die Situation von damals. Kinder mussten mitansehen, wie ihre Mütter vergewaltigt und umgebracht wurden. Viele Frauen wurden schwanger, viele geschlechtskrank. Auf Hilfe konnten sie nicht hoffen. Um ihren Peinigern nicht immer wieder in die Hände zu fallen, versteckten sie sich in Wäldern, Kellern und auf Speichern. Das Trauma der erlittenen Gewalt lässt die Frauen bis heute nicht los. "Das kommt in stillen Stunden, abends wenn es ruhig ist, bevor ich zu Bett gehe. Wenn ich mein Abendgebet gesprochen habe, dann kommt das, wenn ich ganz alleine bin," bekennt Christel Jolitz, deren leidvolles Schicksal sich kaum in Worte fassen lässt.

NIGHT OF TERROR

Within hours after the Americans withdrew, Stalin's hordes crossed the Elbe and entered the town. The Russians' approach could be heard a long distance in advance because of their drunken clamor that emanated from trumpets and assorted musical instruments they had looted along the way. They traveled in open horse wagons loaded with feed sacks and looted goods. Occasionally Russian military women sat among the men. Their appearance was unusually homely. Dressed in uniforms consisting of drab quilted jackets with a leather belt around the waist made them look extra plump. The most unattractive feature was the women's hair style, each a blunt cut at the jaw line and, to keep the hair from falling into their bloated faces, a large aluminum comb stuck at the crown of their heads held it in place. Some of the carts had cows and sheep tied at the end, plundered livestock to be slaughtered as needed. I was surprised to also see underneath some of the Soviets' carts mongrel dogs trotting along between the rear wheels.

Trailing this motley gang was another unit of Stalin's invasion troops. Like a scene from Genghis Khan, riding small, trotting steppe horses, they were exotic Mongolians with drooping beards, scimitars at their sides and guns strapped across their backs. Sounding like a traveling circus, the Russians decided to make camp for the night, which meant they were going to take over the town, break into farms and homes.

As the sun settled over Oschatz, we heard the firing of machine guns. Screams of women and the Russians' high-pitched voices left the villagers in a paralysis of terror. Characteristic of their style of military campaign, they relied on procuring their supplies along the way through plunder. Soviet invasion troops imposed a trail of terror upon civilians where ever they advanced into Germany. They stole anything edible, as well as fresh horses and livestock. They entered houses to look for alcohol, cuckoo clocks, musical instruments, and anything of mechanical nature. They yanked water faucets out of the walls, expecting to take back with them to Russia the convenience of running water. Radios and sewing machines were among the most prized loot they could load on their horse carts. They violently grabbed watches from the wrists of Germans and lined them up, as many as six in a row, on their own arms. The Soviets gang-raped women, from grandmothers to little girls. Family members who tried to intervene, were shot in cold blood.

The night the Soviets arrived, my mother and I were trapped inside a room on the second floor of the house whose elderly owners had taken us in on the same day we had arrived. The house was located on the main street of Oschatz. The room across the hall was occupied by a woman and her twelve year old son, whom I had be-friended only the day before the Soviets arrived. Egmar Beck had lent me his English pocket dictionary which we used to read the American paperback book I had found in the abandoned handcart. Now, with the Soviets roaming the village, to flee from our room or to be on the street in the dark would be deadly.

My mother worried about my brother and my father at the stables across the street, where our horses were boarded. Soviets usually shot on sight all German men who were six feet and above, in their presumption that they were members of the Waffen SS. Ernst was six feet two, however he was a paratrooper – not a member of the SS.

Under the circumstances, my mother and I shared the single bed in the small room, but we were too frightened to fall asleep. As the hours passed, screams in the distance and sporadic shots echoed through the night. Suddenly, a loud banging on the downstairs door of the house culminated into the crashing noise of the door being broken down.

Russians entered the lower part of the house, with their high-pitched voices screaming "Uhri! Uhri! – Schnapps! Schnapps!" (German words, demanding "watches" and "liquor.") A burst of shots rang out, and we heard the elderly woman's cries of anguish.

By now, my mother had jumped out of bed and, with a voice tense as I had never heard her before, she whispered, "Close your eyes and do not resist if the Russians attack you..." With that, she flung the featherbed over me in an attempt to hide me. As I peeked through a narrow opening from under the pillow I saw my mother, in her state of panic, put on top of her nightgown my overcoat, the only garment within her reach. Being too small for her, the tight sleeves pulled her arms back and left her looking helpless in a grotesque way. She had no time to change, when loud voices and the sound of boots on the stairs approached our room. Frightened, I quickly closed my peek-hole under the cover and I heard the door fly open. The high-pitched, terrifying voices screamed, "Uhri, Uhri, Schnapps!"

It was only a moment before I felt my cover being thrown aside and two drunken Russians looked down on me. One wore a black leather jacket and held, at hip level, a sub-machine gun. The other was taller and wore the typical Soviet tunic and a fur cap with dangling ear flaps. Looking for Schnapps, his attention seemed to be drawn to the credenza along the wall, and he walked over to yank open the drawers. When he found them locked, he furiously grabbed my mother, shouting for her to open them. Gesticulating frantically, she succeeded in making him understand that she did not have a key.

Horrified about the other Russian at the side of the bed holding the gun to my head and, with his other hand, beginning to fidget on his clothing, my mother's reaction seemed bizarre when she pulled from her purse my student pass with my picture. Holding it in front of the Russians's face, she tried to show him that my age was listed as sians's face, she tried to show him that my age was listed as only thirteen years old. Just then, the most unexpected happened. Perhaps the scene had become too surreal even for these barbarians, when the taller Russian, who apparently was of a higher rank, suddenly began to slap the one by the bed from behind across the head. Shouting, he shoved him and his machine gun to the door. Still pummeling him, they both left the room. Immediately, we heard them going across the hall to enter the room of Egmar and his mother. Then I heard the Russians close the door behind them and I recognized Egmar's voice screaming, screaming...

Hurriedly, we dressed and my mother opened the window. In the dark, we lowered ourselves onto the roof of a lean-to. From there, we climbed on a stack of fire wood and jumped to the ground. We spent the rest of the night lying flat in a flowerbed behind a low privet hedge about thirty feet from the house. It was pitch-dark, and we listened for any sounds. We froze in terror when, in the adjoining yard, the glow of a cigarette appeared and we heard a man clear his throat. Suddenly a spot light began to sweep slowly back and forth across the garden. With our faces pressed against the ground, the beam of light skimmed inches above our heads. We barely breathed. I don't recall how long we laid on the ground.

Next morning, I discovered that a garden trough near the privet hedge behind the house was filled with water that was tinged bright red. A blood-stained oriental rug was soaking in it. We learned that, when the Russians had entered the downstairs of the house shouting "Uhri Uhri," the old man, responding to their demands for watches, pointed at a "Regulator," a carved clock that hung on the wall of his living room. That's when the Russian in the leather jacket machine-gunned him down. I never found out what happened to Egmar Beck and his mother across the hall from our room.

FROM THE ATTIC

My mother and I were worried what may have happened to my father and Ernst during that night. We had no further encounter with the Soviets, and the town seemed quiet with the beginning hours of an uncertain day, and we managed to cross the street to the farmyard, where they had stayed overnight with the stabled horses. We were relieved to find my father unharmed. He immediately sent us upstairs to the attic of the farmhouse. There, we found Ernst and another German soldier, a man in his late fifties, and several girls and adult women, who were hiding from the Soviets.

Ernst quickly described the events of the previous evening when the Soviets entered the farmyard. Drunk from the plundered schnapps, they yelled and kept shooting their guns into the air. When the Soviets found Ernst and a young German soldier, whom Ernst had only met that day, they pushed both at gunpoint against the wall of the stable. Then they ordered them to remove their jackets and raise their arms. Waffen SS members routinely wore in their armpit a tattoo, which indicated their blood type. Ernst had never seen one before and was terrified when he noticed that this young fellow's armpit was tattooed. Knowing that Soviets killed SS members, he feared that in their unruly state they would also shoot him.

Just then, loud voices distracted everybody when several other drunken Soviets had found the farmer's motorbike in a shed. They pushed it into the yard where they repeatedly failed to start it up. While everybody became occupied with the motor bike, and the Russians grew louder and more enraged with each attempt to start it, Ernst managed to point out that the sparkplug was missing and that he would get one. In their frenzy, one shot at his feet, signaling him to hurry and bring a sparkplug. Of course, Ernst had no idea where to find a sparkplug, nor the intention to bring one, but he used the opportunity to leave the scene. He ran behind the barn and entered the farmhouse from the backdoor to rush into the attic. That's why we found him there that morning. We never learned what happened to the hapless young German with the tattoo in his armpit.

At midday the farmer's wife, dressed in baggy rags and a babushka in an attempt to repel Soviet rapists, brought us some bread, smoked bacon and a pail of water from her kitchen. She was very upset and reported that Erika had been gang-raped during the night, and that her father was injured from a gun wound.

We cowered in fear, and nobody spoke. By late afternoon, I again heard gunfire from the farmyard below and the high-pitched voices of drunken Soviets. Carefully, Ernst lifted a roof tile to peer through a narrow opening. I could tell that he was becoming increasingly agitated.

I stepped up and, straining to reach the open gap, I saw my father standing in the middle of the yard in front of two horses that were hitched to the Soviets' wagon. I was puzzled why he kept picking up the same handful of hay to hold in front of them as if to feed them, and then he dropped the hay, only to pick it up again and again, repeating the futile routine. That's when I noticed that my father kept his eyes fixed on somebody who sporadically fired a submachine gun into the air, but who was not visible from my vantage under the tile roof.

All of a sudden, my father's head turned as a Russian appeared to his side where I could finally see him. The Russian had the weapon aimed directly at my father. And the submachine gun did not go off! Evidently it was overheated by then.

My father's face was like stone when he reached for the gun with a gesture of trying to examine it. He gingerly took it from the drunken Soviet's hand. Raising it calmly into the air, he pulled the trigger and emptied the magazine with a burst of shots.

*Advancing Soviets in eastern Europe (left),
German Soldiers' grave in the USSR (right).*

Mongolians in Germany, 1945

wwwwwwwwwwwwwwwwwww

PEDESTRIANS

We remained in hiding for several more days. Finally one morning the Soviets were gone – and so were our horses. They had taken them, along with the carriage. Perhaps one of their commissars longed to ride in it. Josef, too, had disappeared – he may have decided to return to Poland.

We finally were able to leave the attic. The street, that had been crowded with refugees and released POWs before the Soviets' arrival, was now quiet. The hand cart, that I had salvaged after the American POW had abandoned it on the road, became suddenly important when we loaded it with some of our belongings, the rest and the sack with smoked meats we strapped on a second cart, this one had only two wheels. Still trying to reach safety from the Soviets, we needed to continue our trek. The alternative was to become trapped behind what would become known as the Iron Curtain. Our next goal was to cross the river Mulde, which was located on a southwest course about fifty miles from Dresden. This would put us into the direction toward Nuremberg.

Definitive borders that would eventually divide the American from the Soviet Occupation Zones were not yet in place, and we were uncertain whether we might encounter the Soviets again.

By late afternoon we reached Colditz, where we crossed the river Mulde. There too, the bridge was damaged by bombs – however this time it had been repaired, perhaps by American forces before they withdrew from the Soviets. Having walked about three miles west, after crossing the bridge, we encountered several Germans on bicycles who stopped to ask how we had managed to get across the Mulde, because when they got to the river, the Soviets had blocked the bridge, and they were no longer able to reach their homes. Once again we were lucky to have crossed a river just in time.

The following days were taken up by the tedium of a hundred steps leading into two hundred more steps, while pulling the carts. Trying to stay away from large cities, we walked on country roads through villages, which lead to the incident when, toward the last farmhouse, Ernst threw his jacket on a screeching chicken which we cooked and ate that night somewhere along the way. Another day, a young man showed up to join us. He fashioned a sling from a rope and, putting it over his shoulder, he helped pull one of the

Dresden, 1945 (left), Nuremberg, 1945 (right).

carts. I recall that I found it disturbing that he had a missing front tooth – otherwise he would have been handsome. He may have been a German soldier whose unit had disbanded before the advancing enemy. The term "deserter" at this stage of the war made no sense. And yet, the fear that some-body might question his being around and alive may have motivated him to blend in with a refugee family. I don't re-member when or where he left our company – perhaps when he had reached the proximity of his family's home.

Each night we stayed in different barns or farms. In one instance, trying to sleep in an attic, the cooing of pigeons in the gable kept us awake. Again, Ernst's dexterity created a momentary chaos in the coop when his hands groped and caught several pigeons, which we ate the next day.

After about eighty miles on country roads, and skirting the city of Chemnitz, a major industrial center which lay in rubble from bombing raids, we reached the area of Zwickau. There we entered a ramp to the Autobahn where, before us, the vast super highway extended into the horizon without a vehicle in sight. That's when we, four people pull-ing two handcarts, accompanied by our wire terrier Murrax, walked for a day on the Autobahn, the Nazis' historic hall-mark of highway engineering. The smooth concrete surface gave us much relief. In fact, when the road turned into a long downhill stretch, Murrax and I perched on the Ameri-can POW's handcart and, steering the handle with my feet, I coasted with ease and enjoyed the breeze in my face. I was having fun!

After hours of tedious miles on the concrete band of road through the state of Saxony, we approached an enor-mous viaduct and were stunned to find that halfway across the span a large section had been blown up, either by re-treating German forces, or some well-aimed Allies' bombs. A bus, the most modern bus I had ever seen – and it looked brand new – was wedged, head-first into a twenty-foot wide bottomless crater. The bus was empty. Hard to tell how long

ago it had come to this catastrophic stop, and how many people were hurt by the impact. To our everlasting gratitude somebody had left, next to the bus and across the gaping hole, two heavy planks of timber, each about one foot wide. When I stepped up to the edge I felt dizzy. In the distance below the viaduct was an entire village. With great risk, my father and Ernst adjusted the two pieces of wood into parallel tracks so that they would accommodate the wheels of the carts.

Overwhelmed by the height of the viaduct and the size of the gap before me, I froze in panic. It took considerable coaxing by my parents before I finally put my feet on the swaying planks to cross the yawning abyss.

FIRST IMPRESSIONS

It was late and we were tired when we decided to spend the night at the side of a railroad embankment. Ernst gathered a few branches and rocks to build a fire. In the sack with the hard salami were several potatoes from the farm where we had stayed the night before and, as usual, we used the skillet to fry the food. Later, we curled up in blankets but the cool air kept us from getting much sleep.

At daybreak, the sound of a freight train pulled by a steam locomotive broke the silence. It approached slowly and gradually came to a stop to wait for a switch. We quickly packed our blankets on the two hand carts, and, holding Murrax tightly under my arm, I climbed on top of an open flatbed filled with gravel. The train began to move again and Ernst hurriedly helped my parents lift the two handcarts on the rail car. Riding a train would be a great relief after weeks of walking. I panicked suddenly when I noticed the rail cars began to speed up as they rolled by Ernst's lonely figure standing on the side of the embankment. What if he were left behind? "Ernst, get on the train! Get on the train!" I screamed in terror. As the train picked up speed, he grabbed the last handrail in his reach and pulled himself up the steps of the caboose, the very end of the moving train. The idea of riding a caboose could be funny, but it was not.

It was the beginning of May and four months since we had fled Poland during a January blizzard. Now, we finally felt safe from the Soviets because we knew that we had reached the American Occupation Zone. We were not quite sure whether this freight train would take us to Furth or Nurnberg. As the hours passed, perched on top of the white gravel, I marveled how easily the countryside slid by the train, so much faster than during the weeks when we had to walk, pulling the two handcarts. Some days, when we did not encounter hills that made the carts heavy, we had actually managed to walk over twenty kilometers before night fall.

Suddenly, screeching brakes brought the train into a slow crawl. Loud voices and a flurry of uniforms surrounded us. American soldiers with MP armbands had boarded the freight train. Before we knew what was hap-

pening, our wooden handcarts loaded with our few belongings were being thrown over the side of the train, where they tumbled down the embankment. I saw a wheel spin crazily into the air and our bundles rolled upon the ground. One of the soldiers grabbed my mother's arm shouting: "Raus, raus!" as he pushed her to the edge of the moving car. Ernst, reacting to the angry American soldiers, jumped off the caboose at the rear and raced toward the side of the gravel flatbed, where he caught my mother, just as she was about to fall. My father was already on the ground, and I quickly jumped off the train with Murrax following me in a long leap. The GIs returned to their parked jeep and disappeared. The train resumed its journey…

DONAUWOERTH

After the American military police had thrown us off the moving gravel train, it took a while to gather our scattered belongings from the embankment. As I suspected, the wheel that I had seen fly through the air had come from one of our two carts. Ernst discovered that the axle was broken from the impact. We managed to move its content onto the remaining cart, the one with only two wheels.

Now that it was piled with our bundles twice as high as it had been before, we were concerned that, under the added weight, it might break down – ironically after months of fleeing from the Soviets, just as we had reached safety in the American Occupation Zone.

Pushing the heavy cart, we continued our trek on the dusty country road along the side of the rails. By having ridden on a freight train for a few hours, we had lost track of where exactly in West Germany we were. The day began to warm under a full sun and I was not feeling well, I had several urgent calls that took me behind bushes. Considering that we had not had adequate food for weeks, perhaps these were symptoms of some gastric disorder. An area below my right ribs felt painful, and I thought I could actually hear a gurgling sound when I took a deep breath.

After walking for a while, we saw a road sign that read "Donauworth, 2 km." My father recognized the name as a small Bavarian town near Ulm, and he recommended that we find a farm or a barn to stay there overnight. Since we were slowed down pulling the heavy cart, he walked briskly ahead of us to look for a place where we could stay. An hour later when we entered the town, we noticed that it must have been bombed recently. There were smoldering ruins and the main street was lined with rubble. Instead of houses and barns, the few remaining walls invited the eye to gaze through empty windows into the open sky above. We found my father waiting for us at the side of the road and he led us toward the edge of the village where several farms had escaped the bombs. We entered a gate into a yard where a woman met us in the door of the farmhouse. She showed us to an upstairs room with several straw mattresses on the floor, and my mother immediately made sure that I lay down. I again noticed the gurgling sensation under my ribs. Before I fell asleep, she brought me a cup of peppermint tea from the farmer's kitchen.

I don't know how long I slept, but I felt better when I awoke. It was midday and I was hungry. The farm woman – being helpful – invited my mother to look for eggs in the hen house and she gave us a loaf of bread. I continued to rest and, by afternoon, Ernst and I walked to the nearby fields to search for food – for potatoes or rutabaga. In the middle of a field we came upon a mound of dirt, and we suddenly realized we were surrounded by bomb craters, each filled with brown water. Ernst bent down to pull on what appeared to be a boot sticking up from the loosely thrown up soil. With horror, he dropped it when he found a man's leg attached to it. Just then I saw in front of me a human hand extending from the dirt of the crater. The palm was turned toward the sky as in a gesture of submission. We hurried back to the village.

Later, we learned that Donauworth used to be the home of a factory that made farm machinery, and that the plant had been converted to produce Stuka parts during the war. Because of labor shortage, American prisoners of war from a nearby camp worked at the factory. Only a few days earlier, on April 11, 1945, over a hundred B-17s had bombed the factory. When, with the sound of air raid sirens, the POWs fled from the buildings, the Allies – seeing running people – carpet-bombed the field, leaving it to resemble a moonscape with hundreds of dead American POWs.

Next morning, while trying to help the farm woman, I met a girl in her kitchen. She was a little older than I and very pretty – her name was Heide. She wore a thin pink blouse and her blonde hair was curled around her shoulders and held in place with a velvet ribbon. She told me that she was fourteen years old. From her I learned that Donauwoerth was occupied by soldiers who were Philippine-Americans, and that they gave her chewing gum and chocolate bars. Out of a shoulder bag she pulled a brown-and-gold wrapped chocolate bar. "See?" she said. "Here, try it, I have some more in my carton in the barn." With that, she broke a piece off and gave it to me. I had not tasted chocolate like this before, it melted like warm gold inside my mouth. "The American soldiers are very nice," she said. "Do you want to see where my house was?" she asked. "Come with me and I'll show you."

We walked a short distance through the bombed village. I saw no people, but noticed the stench of dead animals. We entered what used to be a farm. Every building was leveled into piles of rubble except, at the end of the yard, the remnants of a barn were still standing. "That's where I sleep, in the barn," she said, adding, "There's plenty of straw, and I have an army blanket to keep warm."

After climbing over loose timber and piles of brick, she stopped in front of a gaping hole and we looked down into the open cellar of what used to be a house. Her hand pointing at a heap of rubble in the corner of the foundation, Heide said softly, "My Papa and Mama are down there."

JOACHIM !

Without the threat of the Soviets at our heels, we began to relax. No more carts to pull for miles, and we were able to rest and recover our strength. It was obvious that the war was coming to an end. Bombardments ceased and the only military we saw in Donauwoerth were occasional Americans in Jeeps and trucks. Food was terribly scarce. We ate lots of potatoes and rutabaga soup. These large yellow beets were grown by farmers to feed cattle.

Everyday we worried about Joachim, where he was, whether he was alive. Just like in the case of Ernst, the last letter we had received was before Christmas of 1944, a few weeks before we left Poland. Last we knew, Joachim was stationed in Hungary. There he served as a radio operator with a Junkers 87, "Stukas," unit. We knew that something needed to be done. Because Joachim did not know where we were, my father announced one morning that if the rails were intact, he will take a train to Freilassing. His reasoning was that, just like Ernst try-

1944, Joachim, 18 yrs., Luftwaffen member

1938 Kamml's farm house in Freilassing

ing to find us in Falkenberg, Achim in his case, might be looking for us in Freilassing. If he escaped from Hungary, Freilassing would be his first choice on the basis of geography, as well as our family's past connections.

Going back to the time of my father's office as mayor of Freilassing, a farmer by the name of Ludwig Kamml was his agricultural commissioner for the area. Above all, the Kammls were close family friends. During school vacation, my brothers and I, as a seven-year-old, spent wonderful days on their typically Bavarian chalet-type farm, leaving me with fond memories. Among the many visits was one when Grandmother Kamml inspected and made me wash my feet before I was al-

The Kamml Family 1938

lowed to stomp sauerkraut in a large barrel downstairs in the cellar. And never again did I find similar, heavenly prune-fritters, deep-fried in butter, like Frau Kamml made for dessert. We speculated that, if Joachim had escaped from the Russian Front, our past special relationship with the family might lead him to go to the Kamml's. We sent all our prayers with my father when he took a train next morning to search for Joachim in Freilassing.

Two days later, the door opened and Joachim and my father entered the room. To this day I can't explain why I screamed. A frozen agony, suppressed during the weeks of our trek, seemed to dissolve when I saw him. Considering each of our incredible journeys, our family's reunion was a marvel.

I listened with keen interest to his account of how he escaped from Hungary. Due to fuel shortage and the breakdown of logistical support, his Junkers-87 squadron had been grounded since the fall of 1944 and the personnel billeted on private farms. There, during several months, Joachim apparently became like a member of a family, where he participated in farm work characteristic of Hungarian traditions – such as chucking corncobs in the barn – and flirting with the farmers daughter. Eventually, with Stalin's military advance into Europe and the collapse of the Eastern Front, Joachim's unit disbanded by either fleeing or being taken prisoner and shipped to Siberian forced labor gulags. Ultimately, this crisis led the farmer to persuade Joachim to stay, promising that he would hide him as a member of his family, until the Russians were gone, so that later he could marry his daughter.

Joachim's account was filled with warm, personal memories of his life with this family. However, he did not want to become a Hungarian farmer – especially not under Soviet dominance – and he finally decided to leave. He and another soldier took off and made their way back to Germany through the snow of the Carpatian Mountains on foot and by riding on freight trains, whenever they could. Their main concern was not to be discovered as German soldiers. When he finally arrived in Freilassing, the Kammls were surprised to see him, but also overjoyed. After several weeks of waiting without any sign of our whereabouts, Joachim, anxious to find us, was ready to leave the Kammls the next day to search for us in Falkenberg – when my father showed up.

<center>~~~~~~~~~~~~~~~~~~~~~~~~~~</center>

THE MISSED TRAIN CONNECTION

Clearly we could not stay in the bombed out town of Donauworth. The area offered no work for my father and brothers.

Considering the catastrophic shortage of housing in bombed out cities and the even more drastic conditions of famine in urban areas, my mother's advise was to find a new home in Lower Bavaria, around Rosenheim, or Muehldorf. Those towns were in rural areas that were less overrun by refugees and had been spared heavy bombings.

Many rails were destroyed, and few trains were running between towns and cities. Yet, having had success in riding a train to Freilassing, my father was optimistic that he would find a connection to Lower Bavaria.

Soon, he and Joachim embarked on the trip to Muehldorf. After three hours of ride, they missed to change train in Markt Schwaben, as a result they arrived an hour later at an end-station, in a town called Erding, about 35 km north east of Munich. There, they stayed overnight in a Gasthaus.

The next day, they found out that located in Erding was a large American Airbase, where jobs were readily available.

In short, because my father and Joachim having missed to change trains, our new home after WWII was to become Erding...

My Comments, 2004:

Immediately after the war, victims of war, as well as observers, were far more direct and spontaneous with their words. Their memories of experiences were fresh, and evidence visible all around. The mass expulsions of 15 million Germans are part of WW II, and it was the largest migration in human history. Today such crimes are called "ethnic cleansing."

Two million Germans, mostly women and children, perished in the process of these expulsions. It is wrong to trivialize a deed that caused the deaths of two million civilians through starvation, exposure, violence, atrocities and deadly camp internments as "only" two million – in the sea of deaths. Their deaths are a multiple of all US combat WWII fatalities in both theaters of war, and to the families involved, every person of these two million counts. Incredibly, this tragedy remains nearly unrecorded in WWII history.

I do not subscribe to Stalin's cynical philosophy that the death of one is a tragedy, but the death of a million is a statistic. More importantly, the mechanisms of such outrageous state-sponsored social engineering must be understood – regardless of who did it: Hitler, or Stalin prior to, during, and after the war. – In the case of the Germans' it was with the signatures of the Allies...

Such behavior has to become completely unacceptable. Otherwise bad precedent will lead to repetitions – as it has already in the Baltics, and currently in the Middle East – on a smaller scale. It will generate destabilizations and animosity for generations to come. It is not something the world needs. If one justifies ethnic cleansing in one case and condemns it in an-

other, the door is left open for abuse and creative accounting.

In order to avoid misunderstandings, I have not and will not make comparisons to The Holocaust. Yet, it is important to note, that the term "Holocaust" did not exist until after 1952, when it was coined by Elie Wiesel in his novel "Night." And the Holocaust did not begin to reach the formal, crystallized, and almost ritualized stage and cultural world-wide impact, until after Israel's Six Day War...

There is a field called "genocide studies" and a body of literature on ethnic cleansing. Serious investigations into the nature and classification of human rights disasters and crimes against humanity require extensive expertise in law and international law, as well as a fair amount of objectivity. De Zayas was one of the (early) investigators of the German expulsions. Other historians, dealing with this and other ethnic cleansings and forced mass deportations, will certainly continue to follow.

Apart from the outspoken activism by prominent figures like Lord Bertrand Russell, ("...in mass cruelty, the expulsions of Germans ordered by the Russians fall not very far short of the atrocities perpetuated by the Nazis;") and Victor Gollancz, ("Our Threatened Values" and "In Darkest Germany") there are many other comments, plus a multitude of reports, accounts, diaries and other documents. Thousands of detailed interviews with refugees and expelled persons were conducted at the time by the German authorities in the West. They are now waiting in the archives.

MAP OF GERMANY AFTER WWII
FOUR MILITARY OCCUPATION ZONES

To escape the approaching Soviets, our trek by horse carriage began during a blizzard on January 21, 1945 in Dolsk, south of Posen (Poznan), Poland. We crossed the Oder in Guben, south of Frankfurt. From there, on the way to Falkenberg, we saw Dresden burn on February 13. We stayed for several weeks in Falkenberg, between Berlin and Torgau. Ernst arrived in Falkenberg from a military hospital in Berlin. When Stalin's troops crossed the Eastern Border of Germany, we resumed our trek and crossed the Elbe

in Strehla, south of Torgau on April 25th to reach the American side of the Elbe. In Oschatz, the Americans withdrew and the Soviets arrived and took our horses. From Oschatz, we continued our flight on foot. Dodging air raids, we walked for days, including on the Autobahn, to reach Hof. From Hof, we rode on a gravel train to Fuerth, near Nueremberg. From there, we walked to Donauwoerth and rested for a few days. From Donauwoerth, my father took a train to look for Joachim in Freilassing, 20 kilometers from Salzburg, where he found him. Thankful to be alive and together again, we all left Donauwoerth by train to Munich - Erding where we settled as refugees in June 1945. The total distance of our trek was approximately 420 miles.

V.
Erding

1945 – 1950

ERDING ... our new home town, after an air raid,
few weeks before we arrived in June 1945

A PLACE FOR SECRETS

In June of 1945, we at long last settled in Erding, a small town in Bavaria, about 20 miles northeast of Munich. Our few possessions were in a handcart, but we were thankful to be alive, to have escaped the Soviets, and to be together as a family. The local refugee agency assigned us a four-room cottage, where the kitchen had a woodstove and in the entrance hall was a hand pump. In the backyard, stood a tidy outhouse. We felt very fortunate with these conditions because the alternative could have been one of the many camps, where millions of refugees languished for years after the war.

Just having turned into a teenager, the postwar famine and poor living conditions deprived me of any exploration of fashions or cosmetics – I did not even own a pretty dress. It was my good fortune, however, when my father succeeded in getting for me an old upright piano through the postwar bartering system in exchange for a truckload of firewood. This meant I was able to resume practicing Schubert, Beethoven and Bach – they represented a form of continuity to what I had known and loved before the calamities of war had broken up our lives. Being new in this small town, I had no friends, and I was lonely...

As the summer passed, I one day discovered an intricate ecosystem in the outhouse. In its unspeakable abyss, there were lively maggots, which I resisted watching too closely. Inside the corner of the slanted roof, however, I saw a beautiful web that belonged to a garden spider. When I gently touched the fine gossamer threads, the spider reacted like lightening and rushed into the net from its hiding place. This cunning behavior intrigued me, and I caught a fly to throw into the middle of the web. Instantly the spider rushed to wrap the hapless victim into a tasty morsel. I continued the routine of feeding the spider for the rest of the summer and the spider grew to be plump. Still, I despised her looks.

With the approach of winter, the first hard frost killed the spider, and I was relieved that this symbiotic relationship ceased and that the spider's death ended my secret in the outhouse...

CHRISTMAS 1945

By the time I turned fourteen, everything I had known up to this point in my life had changed. My playful childhood in Poland had come to a brutal halt when we fled from the advancing Soviets. Our belongings were gone. My mother, a woman with extraordinary talents, now went to Bavarian villages to barter her homemade blouses for food. Moreover, my father's image as a man of calm authority, a civil servant during the Third Reich, was now reduced to being a gardener at an American military base.

In 1945, US Occupation Authorities initiated a "De-Nazification Program" in the form of hearings and trials. In addition, the US Military Information Service operated "Re-education Programs" that focused on German schools and universities – the program confiscated, edited and screened textbooks, and controlled the German media.

Because of the Nazi period, my father had become a man without a past – nor future. After 1945, a German who had held any administrative position during the Nazi period, whether as school superintendent, title-holding athlete, chief surgeon, police chief, opera director or scientist, millions were subject to post-war "De-Nazification Investigations." For this purpose, over 600,000 Germans were in detention camps under starvation conditions, operated by US Military Occupation forces, awaiting their turn.

To delay – or avoid – recognition, my father reversed his names from Adolf R. to Robert A. Koppe on his registration form in Erding's refugee office. Even though he had been a small wheel in the Nazi bureaucracy, he, as millions of other administrators who worked during Hitler's reign, was subject to arrest by the De-Nazification authorities, to be held for months in one of the many detention camps – in some cases, for years. The hearings were intended to determine whether the individual had committed any war crimes. Being confident of not having committed any crimes, and considering the loss of our assets, he opted for the alternative – namely to risk the penalty for anonymity as long as possible, so he could support the family and help Ernst get his engineering degree at the university in Munich.

By 1952, the backlog in De-Nazification hearings had subsided and my father reported his past civil service position under the Reich to the authorities. That is when his original idea paid off because his hearing took place immediately. In fact, after routine investigations, he was commended by the Denazification Commision for having secretly tipped off the only Jewish family in Freilassing, (risking his own safety) – where, as mayor in 1938, he had been ordered to turn over the names of the town's Jewish residents under a Nazi census program. Because of his efforts at that time, this Jewish family left for Austria and escaped the war. They testified in behalf of my father.

The mass expulsions of Germans from Eastern Europe at the end of the war led to an immeasurable tragedy affecting generations. Millions of families were separated. For years, in an attempt to reunite them, the Red Cross aired hours of daily search programs on the radio, which cited last known places of the missing persons, family members, missing German soldiers, POW camps, as well as the numerous Siberian forced labor camps. At the time, I was too young to grasp just how fortunate we were, that our family was together, and that my brothers had returned from the war – without injuries.

With WWII over, the images I had grown up with during the Nazi period – from swastika flags to patriotic march music and rallies – were gone. Instead, American Jeeps drove on German streets, and American jazz music played on German airwaves. Cities, rail stations, museums, universities, libraries and landmarks were destroyed; half of Europe – ten nations – had been handed over into Stalin's brutal tyranny, 120 German cities were reduced to rubble, leaving 900,000 German civilians killed in bombing raids, and millions of ethnic Germans disowned and expelled from Eastern Europe. The German economy and its industry were smashed, currency had no value, schools had no books and, because of famine, thousands died. Years later, I learned of

the Morgenthau Plan, which deliberately had created genocidal conditions for Germans – as the outcome of WWII.

*(See James Baque: 1. Other Losses, and 2. Crimes & Mercies. The
Fate of German Civilians Under Allied Occupation, 1944-1950.
Also: John Sack: An Eye for an Eye)*

At the end of 1945, my recollections of the trek to escape
from the Soviets were still fresh. The months, days and nights
on the road with snow crunching under the wheels of the carriage; the pain of my frostbitten legs; the terror when the Soviets caught up with us at the Elbe; the miles of walking, including on the Autobahn, where we crossed the bombed viaduct
on two swaying planks above a gorge with a village below, were
still palpable in my mind. The screaming boy behind the
locked door while his mother was being raped by leather-
jacketed Bolsheviks, rang in my ears. In addition, I shudder to
recall the droopy-bearded Mongols, guns strapped across their
backs, riding small, trotting horses into Germany. I can't forget
the sound of the hissing red-hot shrapnel fragments that show-
ered from the sky; and how surprised I was when thin smoke
swirled from their impact on the ground in front of my feet.

On a snowy night in 1945, Christmas Eve came upon me
like an odd revelation. In the small cottage with frosted windows, the tiled wood stove and the corner bench around the
table, I still was not confident enough to rejoice that we were
alive. The terrifying memories of the war had shattered my
sense of continuity. In my mind, nothing related to the possibility there could ever again be a holiday, let alone Christmas!
Yet, there, on the windowsill of the kitchen, a timid symbol
of good over evil – and hope, stood a tiny Christmas tree.

AMONG RUBBLE

Just as for millions of other refugees in a country shattered by war, our day-to-day survival depended on whether we managed to find some kind of food – mostly through barter or black marketing.

My days began when I woke from sleep on a straw mattress. Never before had I paid attention to what a mattress was made of, until the refugee office provided us a large empty sack of ersatz burlap, a material woven of twine made of recycled paper. Owning this sack, it was then up to us to find a farmer who would give us some oat straw with which to stuff it. To make a good mattress, I learned that oat straw was preferable over rye or barley straw, for its resilience.

The hand pump behind the entrance door of the cottage provided the water to wash myself each morning in an old enamel basin, which stood on a small table next to the tiled kitchen wood stove. Occasionally, to break the chill, I added a dipper of hot water from the stove's small water reservoir. We had no bathroom, let alone a bathtub. With special effort, we sometimes brought the large laundry vat made of zinc into the kitchen to take a sitz bath. "Privacy" was a utopian notion, found only in the outhouse next to the shed in the yard. As each of us started the day, we somehow managed to take turns with fresh water at the basin by the stove, and finish while nobody was around. Before we all went our ways, no one in the family had eaten breakfast.

Every morning my father and Joachim walked six kilometers each way to the American airbase, where they had found work. Joachim, having trained as a radio-operator in the Luftwaffe, now worked for the American military at the communications shop as a radio technician. Meanwhile, my father became a gardener. He tended the flowerbeds around the American flag in front of the base's headquarters. The main benefit of his work was he had access to the mess hall discards where, every evening before returning home, he filled two buckets on a handcart with swill, including leftover donut batter, for our "black pig." Despite its pink color, it was called a "black pig" because it was kept secretly in a shed behind the cottage – where it was doomed to be slaughtered someday in a hush-hush way by a butcher who, in exchange for a side of bacon, agreed to be in on the secret. After the war, the word "black" had the implication that it was illegal, as in "black market." It meant that, if somebody had turned us in for hiding a "black pig" in our shed, we all would have lost our ration cards – and some other penalty, which I cannot recall now.

We referred to the Americans as "Amis," and my father and Joachim had good relations with Amis; in fact, they had made friends with several of them. Joachim's skills, especially, were in high demand. He was able to barter radio parts or cigarettes with GIs in return for not just fixing their radios and the new trend of installing car radios, but actually building radios for them from scratch. My father, in addition to his gardening job at the air base, reverted one day to his past skills as a military musician in the Kaiser's Heavy Cavalry and his ability to play several instruments, when he founded a jazz band. With instruments furnished by the USO for his six-member band, he played popular American tunes, alternating between saxophone and double bass, most Friday and Saturday nights at the Officers Club. Through his band, he gained access to food, leftover occasionally from parties, which he brought home late at night, in addition to being paid with cartons of Pall Mall or Chesterfield cigarettes for each engagement. Cigarettes had become the purest form of currency; in 1945, they bought most necessities on Germany's black market.

Every morning, Ernst left on a commuter train to lay bricks all day at the Munich Polytechnic Institute, part of Munich's University, which had been demolished in bombing raids. In order to be eligible for admission, he first had to lay bricks one semester for each semester he attended.

Empty restaurants, that had escaped bomb damage, were temporarily used as classroom space. That is when Ernst sat one entire semester on a windowsill in a "Gasthaus," because there were not enough chairs.

Before I went to the nearby high school each morning, I had to do several chores that began with milking the goat in the small shed, a ritual I had to repeat in the evening. Because of my childhood in Poland where I had many pets to play with, I was the only one in the family who knew how to milk a goat. For five packs of cigarettes, a farmer had given my father the goat. I also had to clean out the stack of rabbit hutches and feed the bunnies grass and dandelion leaves, which I gathered along the side of the road. The bunnies too, were destined to eventually provide meat for us. Whenever my mother served a roasted rabbit, which my father had done in (while nobody was looking), there usually was a glum silence at the table.

Our postwar lifestyle was totally new for us. In 1945, German everyday existence had regressed to near Stone Age. No stores could be found, let alone merchandise or food to stock shelves. People stood in long lines in front of a few places designated to distribute certain rationed foods. One such item was yellow-colored bread, baked of American corn meal. We had never seen yellow bread made of cornmeal before. To get milk or butter occasionally, long lines formed in front of some undamaged building with a door open by the sidewalk for a few hours a day. There, milk was ladled into a container which we had to bring ourselves, and tablespoon-amounts of butter were distributed in exchange for a ration card stamp; fifty grams a person per week!

There were no newspapers. Presses had been confiscated and publishers were in detention on orders of US military occupation edicts. Money had no value – therefore, banks were closed. In most towns, libraries, hotels, hospitals, museums, churches, schools, bridges, castles, train stations and peoples' homes lay in ruin, and only few streets were cleared of rubble to allow emergency traffic and pedestrians to get around. In larger cities like Munich, a few trolleys were beginning to operate again in several sections of town, where the streets had been cleared of bombing debris.

Left: BERLIN, *people walking among rubble.*
Right: *MUNICH amid rubble a funeral procession. no streetcars, no transportation. In background the landmark FRAUEN KIRCHE*

During these miserable conditions, my mother turned out to be the most resourceful of us all. Her background as an opera singer, who had sung at the La Scala and at the Royal Court Theater in Munich during the time of Bruno Walter, were utterly useless during a time of famine and barter. Yet, she surprised us with her extraordinary talents. When nobody dared to dream of attractive fashions, she created remarkable blouses made of glossy parachute nylon. In an innovative manner, she removed the silky threads from the chute's cords, then flattened and sewed them in parallel rows on brown wrapping paper cut into the shape of the yoke of a blouse. Using the thick silky threads, she joined the flattened cords with fine, decorative stitches. Later, after removing the paper, she added this lacy yoke to the rest of the blouse.

Every week or so, she took several of the blouses to what was called "hamstern." The word "hamster" being the same in German, the term described gathering food by taking things to farmers in exchange. Occasionally, my mother took an entire day to walk up to ten kilometers, taking her blouses, also lovely homemade slippers to villages. By the power of barter with the peasantry of lower Bavaria, she brought home freshly churned butter, bacon and even a smoked ham. Of course, her wonderful sense of humor and the gift of conversation enhanced her endeavors. They made my mother a visitor many farmwomen actually looked forward to seeing. One served her coffee and peach cake, so she would stay a while. The postwar years were times when German city folks bartered even their upright piano for a butchered pig from a farmer. The famine was so severe that bartering a grandmother's heirloom emerald ring for a dozen eggs was considered a successful deal.

One late afternoon, following her return from a hamster-trip to a village with only a small bag of flour and a few spoons of bacon dripping a farmwoman had put into her bowl, my mother sat down exhausted to rest. With built-up resentment, she confided in me: "I am waiting for the day when these peasants have to peddle their butter door-to-door and, even if it's wrapped in tissue and a silk ribbon, I'll close the door on them…"

Our daily lives eventually fell into a pattern of postwar adjustments, most consisted of deprivations and others were unusual… Ration cards supplied for each of us fifty grams of butter per week, also some sugar, marmalade, and bread. Still, the ration cards combined provided only 800 calories a day per person. It was a time when I was often hungry. As a teenager, I was obviously going through growing-spells.

During the late summer of 1945, in exchange for food, I was lucky to find a job harvesting oats on a nearby farm. In those days, the farmer used an old-fashioned sickle to cut the oats, which I helped to tie into bundles with twisted sheaths of straw, leaving them neatly in rows to be picked up later by a wagon, pulled by oxen. Each midday, I also took on a bicycle a basket of food from the farm to the workers in the field, where I stayed afterwards to work alongside them. I often did not get home until after seven o'clock in the evening because I still had to wash the kitchen floor, after doing the family's dishes. In exchange, I was not only fed a big meal each day but, at the end of the week, the farmer's wife gave me a five-pound bag of flour to take home to my mother.

~~~~~~~~~~~~~~~~~~~~~~~~~~~~

BARTER SYSTEM AND THE BLACK MARKET

The year of 1945 was the worst Germans could remember. Because of air bombardment, 70 percent of buildings in major cities lay in rubble or had been declared unsafe for people to live in. Due to the destruction, survivors sought shelter in basements or, often, three or more families lived in one apartment.

The continuous stream of victims of expulsion from the East further compounded the crisis. Many of them were housed in old military barracks, there was a lack of coal, and people were undernourished. In large cities, many starved or froze to death.

My family was fortunate that our trek ended in Erding. Even though this small town too, had been bombed, it had not been overrun by refugees, as so many other West German communities.

To describe the overall cause of the postwar conditions one has to go back to the Roosevelt and Stalin agreement of Teheran in 1943, which led to Germany's territories located east of the Oder and Neisse rivers, to be handed over into Soviet-controlled puppets, like Poland, while the Northern half of East Prussia was annexed by Russia. The end of WWII resulted in half of Europe, ten nations, a population of 100 million helpless victims, being abandoned by the Western Allies into the terror of Stalin's gulag system.

In 1945, the expulsion of the German population from eastern European States created the largest migration recorded in all history. Under Polish annexations of German territories, Breslau, in the Prussian Province of Silesia and Germany's second largest city, was renamed Wroclaw; Danzig, the German Hansa city of Schopenhauer, became Gdansk; and Koenigsberg, the city of Teutonic Knights in 1255 and the birthplace of Kant, became Kaliningrad in 1945 under the Soviets – and, in 1989, renamed "Chojna" when it became Polish.

After 6 years of war, the German population, including refugees, consisted largely of children, women and the aged. Most adult men between 18 and 55 years of age had been killed, thousands disappeared into Soviet camps, Stalin's Siberian forced-labor gulags – and, among the survivors, many were amputees or crippled. These circumstances, in addition to the destruction of all major industry, created a lack of production of goods and the total collapse the economy. And the old Nazi currency (Reichsmark) had no value. Each day, and particularly on weekends, vast hordes of people trekked out to the country to barter for food from farmers. People hiked through the countryside, going from farm to farm, trying to trade their Persian carpet for a bag of potatoes. Often on bicycles, or pushing a baby carriage, or in dilapidated railway carriages from which everything pilferable had long disappeared, on the roofs and on the running boards, hungry people traveled hundreds of miles at a snail's pace to where they hoped to find something to eat. They took their wares, personal effects, jewelry, old clothes, and sticks of furniture – whatever bombed-out remnants they had – and came back with grain or potatoes for a week or two. My mother was among them, when she took the blouses she had made of parachute nylon, and hand-stitched house slippers to farmers within ten kilometers of Erding.

ABOUT "DPs" – DISPLACED PERSONS

Compounding the Germans' desperate state of economy, reduced to a bartering system, foreign DPs, men with pomaded ducktail haircuts, wearing suits, white open shirt collars and expensive-looking suede shoes with stylish, thick crepe soles, stood on street corners, at rail stations or bridge crossings, where they conducted their black market activities. They approached hungry German people to show, secretly, from their pocket the tip of illegal black market goods, such as chocolate bars, ration cards or cigarettes, to trade for jewelry or other valuables. As a result, money – as an exchange for labor or for the purchase of goods – had no meaning for me as a thirteen year old.

US occupation forces, who were supplied with free chocolate and cigarettes and seeing the despair of the German population, generously distributed those – especially to children and to girls. US cigarettes soon became a surrogate currency and, on the emerging black market, most everything was paid for in cigarettes.

Black market goods soon created an all-out bartering system. Accelerating this false economy were the DPs, the foreign "Displaced Persons," who enjoyed considerable advantage over Germans, because they had goods that Germans had no access to. DPs were thousands of East Europeans, who showed up after the war in West Germany. Most were communists, many had been partisan fighters in support of Stalin during the war, and others had been prisoners in Nazi camps, who were liberated by the Allies in 1945.

UNRRA, the United Nations Relief and Rehabilitation Administration, assisted DPs, who were well organized and who congregated in large German cities. To accommodate them, American Occupation Forces confiscated mansions in an exclusive residential section of Munich, which had escaped bombing raids. After expelling the German owners, DPs moved in. Moehlstrasse, in Bogenhausen, known for its magnificent villas, filled with grand pianos, paintings, chandeliers, and oriental rugs, became warehouses for DPs, their contraband goods and black market operations.

By late 1945, under supervision of US Military Information Service, West Germans were allowed to again publish newspapers, and the airwaves resumed German radio news. It is in this connection I recall frequent reports of police raids on the villas in Bogenhausen, operations called "Razzias," which were executed by American Military Police in collaboration with German law enforcement. News reports described repeated arrests of DPs after seizing entire truckloads of stolen American goods, cigarettes, crates of chocolate, nylons, cosmetics, powdered milk, eggs, silk scarves, leather fashions and fur coats – generally merchandise designated for PX stores and commissaries. How these goods got into the hands of DPs, will probably remain forever with the history of closed files of war-profiteering. Beyond these recurrent reports, there were also special raids to recover U.S. military materiel – including entire field hospitals, tents, jeeps, and USO skiing equipment – as well as millions of German food ration cards, entire lorries of coal and other rationed commodities. Several raids also recovered truckloads of stolen artworks from several German museums.

In summary, the "Black Market" was an odious postwar syndrome, exploiting mostly German women and children, helpless, defeated people, during a time when they already suffered famine and homelessness. For these reasons, the Black Market was also illegal. This corruption finally ended with the Currency Reform on Sunday, June 20, 1948. The basic idea was to replace the worthless Reichsmarks with a much smaller number of new Deutsche Mark (DM), the new legal currency. The money supply was therefore diminished substantially. The currency reform, highly complex, caused many people to take a significant loss of their assets. The net result was about a 93 percent contraction in the money supply.

On Monday, June 21 of 1948 – the day after the currency reform – we were astonished that shops were filled with goods we had not seen in years. I suddenly could buy a coat without first filling out the refugee agency's request form. However, now I was not sure whether I had enough of the new DMs to pay for it!

Recalling the transition on the day of currency reform, my father followed the public instructions and took our savings books of worthless old Nazi Reichsmarks to the nearest bank, coming back with forty new Deutsche Marks in cash for each member of our family. That is all we had. Uncertain of what would happen next, whatever comfort we felt was the knowledge that, overnight, everybody else – whether doctor, housemaid, or factory owner – also started with only forty DMs each.

*Left: Famine in shattered cities. **Right**: Reception centers provide for disinfection of the expellees, who often arrived covered with vermin.*

Outside American barracks in Berlin April 1946, American GIs trying to help starving Germans.

THE MARSHALL PLAN

History describes the Marshall Plan as the American means of saving Europe. Ironically, no amount of money could have restored the damage the bombing raids had caused. Whole cities, bridges, landmarks, hospitals, churches, cultural institutions, utilities, galleries, universities and libraries lay in ashes. Not withstanding Hitler's 12 years of Nazi terror, the rubble the Allies left was a monument to the attempt of destroying centuries of German culture.

Contrary to popular belief, the revival of Germany cannot be attributed to the much-touted Marshall Plan because it was not large enough. It was a loan and has been paid back long ago. Moreover, the Marshall Plan was shared by 13 other nations, which even included Great Britain. Despite having suffered the largest destruction of all European nations, Germany's share in the Marshall Plan was the smallest. Germany's cumulative aid from the Marshall Plan and other aid programs totaled only $2 billion through October 1954. Even in 1948 and 1949, when the aid was at its peak, the Marshall Plan amounted to less than 5 percent of German national income. The other 12 European countries – each having received substantially larger portions of aid – had lower growth than Germany. It is of note that, while Germany was receiving this aid, its new constitution (Basic Law) contained directions for the open-ended restitutions to Israel and Holocaust victims (Luxemburg Agreement / Adenauer) as a condition to be ratified by the US Military Occupation Authority. Under these terms, and despite its own devastated economy, beginning in 1952, Germany was forced to pay well over $2 billion to the newly-created Jewish State. From then on, restitutions were not only for Holocaust victims, but also to build the newly-created State of Israel, its infrastructure, seaports, roads and housing – and to finance international Jewish organizations. These payments, which by 2002 reached over $95 billion, are still ongoing. In addition, following WWII, the Allies charged the Germans DM 7.2 billion annually, ($2.4 billion) to occupy their country. Of course, these occupation costs relieved the Germans from paying for their own defense against their enemy, the Soviets…

<hr />

OLIVE DRAB AND AQUAMARINE

Having left Poland in January in advance of the approaching Soviets, I had lost six months of the previous school year. Despite the risk of failing, I decided to enter the successive grade that fall. I was new to the small Bavarian town and discovered its high school had been destroyed in a bombing raid just during the last days of the war. Based on these circumstances, a suburban parochial school became our temporary accommodations. The entire system was a makeshift arrangement. The most ornery complexity was the lack of books. It was not surprising that, after the war, all libraries were either destroyed or closed, and that all textbooks and educational material of the past Nazi regime needed to be purged from the curriculum – certainly books on history or literature. However, I found it unreasonable that the American military Occupation Authorities also ordered the confiscation of books on chemistry, physics, mathematics, foreign languages, and even music.

The lack of books proved to be time-consuming because teachers needed to dictate much of the subject material, which we took down in longhand. Eventually, in order to establish some semblance of curriculum, we were given thermofaxed single or stapled pages of material that had been approved by the occupation forces. Finally, in 1947, re-edited textbooks began to come out and, as a memento of these times, I saved my first postwar history book. Still on my shelf, the inside of the soft cover reads, "Published under U.S. Military Government Information Control, License Nr. USA-E-115."

During the first days at school, I observed that the students in the classroom reflected much of what had happened. Half of Europe, millions of people who were able, had fled from the murderous Soviets and their savage military hordes.

A great number of the teenagers in my 1945 class had come from those East European states, from the Baltic to the Balkans. Their families, mostly ethnic Germans, were expelled from Hungary, Yugoslavia and Rumania, as well as White Russia, Lithuania and the Ukraine. The long braided black hair of several Albanian girls added an exotic touch to the group. In our shabby clothes, we were an unsightly lot. Boys wore old infantry boots and discarded parts of uniforms, and girls from Slavic countries covered their heads with large babushkas and long fringes. The smell of dirty clothes and oily hair wafted through the crowded classroom. Knuckles of the kids' hands often showed bloody cracks, the typical symptom of "Kraetze," a skin infection. I learned only later that this condition is called scabies, a sign of lack of soap and running water in their crowded camps and refugee shelters.

Many of the teenagers spoke inadequate German, and it was painfully comical that we were hardly able to communicate among ourselves. Moreover, I found it puzzling how they expected to meet the foreign language requirements of Latin, French and English, when it would be taught using German!

Compounding these obstacles was the shortage of teachers. Most educators, in addition to administrators, had been members of Third Reich Teachers Associations or similar mandatory professional organizations that, by the postwar rules, rendered them suspect of political affiliations and subject to investigations. For these reasons, many were held in detention camps in accordance with Allied Occupation Laws.

My girlfriend's father, who had been a school principal under Nazi Germany, was held for three years in a camp to await his turn at a "De-Nazification Trial." Additionally, many teachers had become casualties of the war and therefore did not return to the classrooms. These combined factors contributed to the severe teacher shortage, which caused a number of elderly teachers to come out of retirement. Many of them were East European refugees themselves.

We all shared the same type of poverty demonstrated by malnutrition and, despite our wide-ranging ethnic backgrounds, the common misery of hunger integrated us quickly.

After school, I frequently found at home only a slab of hard rye bread, which I wolfed down with a glass of skim milk. The memory of this lingers only because one time we were in possession of several saccharine pills and, when I added one of them to the milk, the sweet taste made the combination with the bread a memorable feast. It was a time when the German word "Ersatz" became part of universal vocabulary. It meant "substitute," and I was firsthand witness to "Ersatz," which was found everywhere. Bran and other nondescript ingredients were added to flour, turning loaves of bread into the shape and weight of bricks. "Ersatzkaffee" was made of roasted barley, which mocked the olfactory senses by suggesting the aroma of Kenyan coffee, and "Ersatztee," tea, brewed of dried apple peel, was surprisingly tasty, hinting of orange pekoe. Then there was "Ersatzmarmelade" made of sugar beets. Margarine, a yellowish paste, was available only through ration cards in increments of 50 grams weekly per person. Nobody knew just what it consisted of, and nobody even wanted to think about it.

Postwar clothing in Germany would be hard to describe by today's norms. Shoes were the most difficult to get. Only through a written application to the refugee central supply agency was it possible to obtain a certificate necessary to get a pair of shoes. Usually the uppers consisted of Ersatz-leather, a paper-based composition; the soles were made of wood or recycled tires; and, if the shoes had laces, they consisted of tightly twisted twine made of paper.

In August that year, I had turned fourteen, an age when teenagers begin to pay attention to their appearance. Yet nothing could have described my frustration more succinctly than when I had to wear to school an olive drab skirt my resourceful mother had made for me from a military blanket, and a blouse of American aquamarine parachute nylon. Nothing on this earth clashes more than olive drab and aquamarine. To this day, I avoid those two colors.

ONE SURVIVOR

Because of an extraordinary shortage of high school teachers, my physics and mathematics teacher in the fall of 1945 was a man with unusual credentials; he was a rocket scientist without a job. I knew of his background only because he had become befriended with my father. Dr. Gunther Gnass spent much of his free time with our family. I enjoyed listening to his dialect. Like my father, he was a Saxon, a rarity in Bavaria until after the Second World War when Saxons were among the millions of refugees who flooded into Bavaria to escape from the Soviets. Eastern Germany had become the "Russian Occupation Zone." With a population of 16 million, it was to remain buried under Soviet oppression behind the Iron Curtain for nearly fifty years of the Cold War.

Dr. Gnass was a tall man with broad shoulders, and he was in his mid-thirties. Retrospectively, if I had to design a poster of what later depicted the notorious "Aryan super race" of the Nazi period, his physical image, profile, blue eyes, blond hair and tall posture, could have set ideal standards. Despite enormous difficulties as refugees, we shared with Dr. Gnass the good fortune of not being in one of the crowded camps scattered throughout the American Occupation Zone, where millions of homeless people languished for years due to lack of housing.

Dresden – the burnt-out city

Dr. Gnass had left Dresden two days before the historic firebombing of the city on February 14, 1945 when he was on his way to return to Peenemünde. Not only did he escape the bombing and the firestorm in Dresden, but he also escaped serving in the German military. Under normal circumstances, it would have been unheard of that a man of his generation never wore a uniform, considering toward the end of the war even fourteen year old boys were drafted to fight the Soviets.

On Sundays, Dr. Gnass often visited to play chess with my father, and I believe he also liked to visit us because we had a piano – a most extraordinary possession amid the ruins of postwar Germany when people lacked the bare essentials. So that I could continue my music studies, my father had acquired the piano through a black-market deal when he traded a truckload of old lumber in exchange for the piano. It had belonged to an elderly widow, who desperately needed firewood for her stove. I have no idea how my father came into possession of the truckload of wood. It was just another barter deal, because money was worthless.

When Dr. Gnass sat at the piano, I loved to watch his large hands move across the keys. I admired his inventive chord progressions as he improvised, and I envied him so much because I felt limited in being able to play only Bach, Mozart, Clementi, and just a few Schubert pieces. As I stood beside the piano, it was a mystery to me how he pivoted through complex harmonic modulations and I begged him to show me, "How did you get just now from the key of G into A-flat minor?" He stopped for a moment to think. "You must keep playing your Mozart and Clementi, Gudrun." he said, "I wish I could play their music. Keep in mind, unlike you, I never had piano lessons." He smiled wistfully as he continued his improvisations of "C'est Si Bon," one of the recent post war pop-tunes. I concluded that his approach to music was a form of exploring the rules of harmony – not unlike his approach to the laws in physics – and that music making was, for him, simply another discipline. Music was his private passion.

Dr. Gnass, a physicist, was a former member of Wernher von Braun's team in Peenemünde. His work there had exempted him from military service during the war, and its classified nature prompted him to flee before the advancing Soviet troops. It was a time when the Soviets kidnapped hundreds of his fellow scientists and forcibly took them to the interior of Russia, to the Eastern Shores of the Black Sea, where the Soviets created a colony of German scientists for the purpose of ballistic missile research.

Occasionally, Dr. Gnass stayed for dinner or a game of chess with my father. He seemed drawn to our family. We knew he had lost his wife and two children in the Dresden bombing, but he never spoke about it. Once, in a conversation, he confided in us his anxiety of still being on the Soviets' list of German scientists. In fact, he mentioned recent kidnappings, as well as several arrests in the American Occupation Zone by the ALSOS commando of General Patch's 7th Army Operations. It was well known that nuclear physicists, experts on ballistics, aerodynamics and jet propulsion, were being divided between the victorious Allies since the end of the war. Among them were the nuclear scientist and Nobel Laureate Professor Hahn, Heisenberg and Strassman.

"MULTOS ANNOS…"

That same fall, Dr. Gregor Bernatzky became my new Latin teacher – and I disliked him instantly. He looked like an elderly gas-meter reader with a vest. Due to the post-war shortage of teachers, he was among those who had come out of retirement to help fill the need. In addition, Dr. Bernatzky was also a refugee. By his slight dialect, I could tell he was from Silesia, one of the German provinces in the East that, at the end of the war, were abandoned by the Allies into the hands of the Soviets. As a refugee, Dr. Bernatzky's personal appearance showed he, too, suffered from the lack of everyday necessities – including clothing – as we all did. Almost daily, he wore the same baggy suit, evidence he had also lost considerable weight. One morning, he entered the classroom in a flesh-colored shirt under his suit jacket that, for a moment, triggered my imagination into the startling impression that he had wrapped a tie around his bare neck.

Dr. Bernatzky was a classical philologist who, for many years, had taught at Breslau University. Here at the high school, when he took over the Greek and Latin departments, he brought into the classroom the university's protocol of addressing us fourteen-year-old students as Miss and Mister. "Fraulein Koppe, would you step up to the blackboard and show us the conjugation of an irregular verb in the tense of plusquamperfect," said he, as he handed me the chalk. His fingers were peculiarly flat, especially the top of his broad nails. He had the habit of stroking his mustache with those flat fingers. I was not fond of the sound of Latin, however I did enjoy translating the text into German and vise versa; the logic of Latin appealed to me. Written tests, however, were always stressful, and Dr. Bernatzky's background as an educator at university level and his paedagogy so merciless, we adolescents reeled under his high expectations and the discipline of a commissar.

I do not recall what the reason was but, one day, to penalize me, Dr. Bernatzky assigned several pages of Cicero for me to memorize within a week. I always had enormous difficulty memorizing and it was, for me, the most dreaded task – whether it involved multiplication tables, chemistry formulas or poetry. My inability to memorize is probably the reason that I never could recite a poem.

The afternoon I went home with Dr. Bernatzky's assignment, I crawled into a quiet corner and, with Cicero on my lap, I mindlessly chanted the text out loud over and over late into the night. Every morning, my first utterances were in Latin. When my mother spoke to me, I responded with a glazed look and quickly left the room – fearful any external stimulus would scramble and dislodge the delicate accumulation of memorized Latin text deep inside whatever brain cells are designated to retain pages upon pages of Cicero. Days passed and my life was on hold with Cicero on my mind from morning to night. And I hated Dr. Bernatzky with his flat fingers.

Finally, the day arrived that I was to recite the chapter of Cicero from memory. That morning, I had loose bowels, and I knew I looked pale and dramatic. When I arrived at school, a friend took me aside, "Guess what? Bernatzky is out with some kind of illness – no Latin today!" In my knees I felt the powerful urge to drop to the floor in a prayer of thanks.

I never recited Cicero, and Dr. Bernatzky never came back to teach Latin again. Instead, he returned into full retirement in his ground-floor apartment near the park. On the side of his window, he mounted a mirror that gave him an expanded view of the street. He became notorious in town for sitting inside with a pencil and paper, where he meticulously recorded everything that passed outside his window. And I remember so well as if it were only yesterday: "Multos annos Graeci Trojan oppugnaverant..." (For many years, the Greeks occupied Troy.)

~~~~~~~~~~~~~~~~~~~~~~~~~~~~~~~~

THE CHOIRLOFT

By the time I turned fifteen, I began to notice that, on weekends, my girlfriends attended soccer games. Soccer is the most popular spectator sport in Germany, and I was puzzled why the girls gushed over knobby-kneed boys full of mud and sweat. I never understood their yelling, jumping up and down, their screeching, and giggling. Their behavior left me at a loss, and I perceived their soccer enthusiasm as a desperate way to get the attention of boys. In retrospect, as a teenager, I generally dismissed boys of my own age as impertinent louts, and was perplexed by what girls could possibly talk about with them. I think the boys sensed my aversion and, fortunately, left me alone. Such foreboding signs could have destined me to become an old maid.

When I turned sixteen, my brothers invited me to my first New Year's party at a Bavarian Gasthaus. As we left, my mother reminded them to bring me home safely. The Gasthaus was crowded, decorated for the evening, and there was live music. In this kind of setting, Germans typically like to sit around checker-cloth tables in mixed groups – talking, telling jokes, singing along with the music, and doing a little "Schunkeln." That's when they sway on their seats with linked arms, which can be as important as getting up to dance. Since Germans have no drinking age, I think I had also some beer with my dinner and, later, somebody opened a bottle of champagne for the occasion. I am fairly certain that, during my first New Year's Party, I acquired a ringing buzz.

At the table, Ernst introduced me to a friend of his, a schoolteacher by the name of Hansi Mayerhofer. That Hansi had bright red hair disturbed me instantly, because my mother once remarked that "redheads" are false. "They can't be trusted," she said. Nevertheless, I decided then that I just would not tell her about Hansi's red hair. It did not take long when I discovered that he was very charming, well educated, and actually handsome with an open smile. Moreover, what mattered to me most, in contrast to those sweaty juvenile soccer boys, Hansi was definitely an adult. When he told me he also was the organist and choir director at Holy Blood Parish, the 17th century church near the city park, he enhanced his image greatly. After all, I also considered myself a serious musician. Later that evening, before my brothers took me back home, Hansi asked if I would meet him at the church the next day because he would like to play the organ for me there. In any case, it was at this New Years party where, at midnight, I was kissed for the first time and when I committed myself to my first date.

Next day, when I arrived at the church, Hansi was waiting for me. In the sunshine, his hair glistened in hues of flaming peach and orange – again this triggered my skepticism about him, especially now in bright daylight, where his hair appeared much too pretty for a man. With visible concern, he explained he had just discovered that the gate to the choir loft inside the tower was locked. He suggested we could climb over the gate. I stepped inside the ancient tower to examine the challenge. Near the entrance, the narrow winding stairs began their steep ascent to the invisible choir loft somewhere inside the darkness. About six steps up into the tower – almost beyond my view around the bend – was a beautiful, heavy wrought iron gate. It was clear we would have to scale the ornate ironwork of the gate from the narrow steps just below in order to continue our way up the rest of the spiral stairs on the other side. I was never good at climbing, but Hansi encouraged me by offering his locked hands as the first step up the gate. This did help and I found that, once across the gate, the stairs on the other side were close to step down on. Hansi was right behind me as we huffed and puffed our way up inside the narrow tower. Finally, we reached a platform where thick ropes hung from the bells above the belfry. At the side of the landing was a low gothic arch with a heavy timbered door that led into the choir loft – and to the old pipe organ.

*Heilig Blut Kirche in Altenerding
(Holy Blood Church)*

With personal pride, Hansi explained some of the organ's technical characteristics, its ancient vintage, how many pipes it had, and that it operated with the aid of bellows behind the console. He disappeared into a dark enclosure where he used two foot treadles to pump air into the bellows. Then he rushed around to the bench, placed his feet on the organ pedals, hurriedly pulled some stops and, with his white hands gliding over the three manuals of keys, glorious music soared through the vaulted ceiling. I then realized that, if Hansi wanted to complete his Buxtehude prelude, it was up to me to step into the dark hole behind the console and pump the pedals to refill the bellows. Never before had I made music inside a dark hole with so much effort. That is when I decided I did not want to stay much longer on this date.

With Hansi leading the way, we began our descent from the choir loft. With some effort, Hansi climbed over the gate first. Following him, I suddenly found myself helplessly perched on the top of the beautiful wrought iron. Hansi stood at least twenty feet below me, and he was unable to reach high enough to be of help. Behind him, the narrow winding stairs disappeared into the deep abyss of the tower. Frozen in terror, I could not move and I began to cry.

I do not recall how I finally got off the wrought iron gate. To this day, I believe Hansi's choir loft triggered my lifelong acrophobia. And my mother was right – one cannot trust redheads!

<center>~~~~~~~~~~~~~~~~~~~~~~~~</center>

THE GERMAN-AMERICAN YOUTH CLUB

Nicky Hartmann was our English teacher at high school. Being proficient in English, she was also the official interpreter for the American Military Headquarters at the Airbase. Nicky Hartmann was probably in her early forties, and she looked American. I think she deliberately chose her nickname to enhance her American image because "Nicky" is not a German name. She was petite and wore fashionable clothes, the type that did not resemble anything available on the German market. Combined with her American nylons, high heels and lipstick, it was obvious she had connections. She clearly emulated what was to become the postwar "American Look."

Her contact with Americans at the base benefited us students when, one day, she brought into class a carton of Readers' Digest magazines – all of the same date – to distribute among us. They may have been shipped and inadvertently never unpacked, or left over on the PX's periodicals rack. Either way – because all high school textbooks of the Nazi period had been banned under military occupation – suitable English-language material was of enormous value to us students. The Readers' Digest was the first American magazine I had ever seen. Miss Hartmann used it in lieu of a textbook for reading aloud in English, to improve our diction, as well as have us translate several of the articles. In the process, I learned about the 1906 earthquake in San Francisco that, according to this Readers' Digest copy, also frightened Enrico Caruso who had appeared in Carmen at the Mission Opera House only a few hours before the disaster. I would have never known of these events otherwise.

As time passed, Miss Hartmann became a very effective liaison between the Americans and the German community. This role included her effort to recruit us students to join the "German-American Youth Club," which was sponsored by the Base Chaplain's Office. This led to my going with a group of students on a trip to an Alpine area – the name of which I no longer recall. We traveled on an American military bus and stayed at a German youth hostel half way up a mountain. That is where, for breakfast, I ate my first American cereal, the kind that comes in small boxes – our sponsors had supplied them. I did not know whether to pour the orange juice on them and drink the milk, or the other way around. I must say the Crispies did not taste like anything, but made a lot of interesting noise in my bowl (now I know they were "Snap-Crackle-and-Pop").

Later that day, I found myself clinging to the side of a bare mountain with the most beautiful view to be had at two thousand feet, but with nothing to hang on to. There was only a single shrub pine, too small and too far away for me to grab in time if the loose gravel under my feet gave way. I screamed. Terrified, my eyes searched for our guide, the GI-volunteer who, instead of watching over us, had egged us on to climb the mountain. He was nowhere in sight. Today I think he was probably a native of Kansas who, via weekly APO letters, wrote his folks about the crazy Bavarians and their exotic passion to climb mountains. Using every fingernail I could muster, I eventually crawled back to safety.

Sometime later, in preparation for Christmas, the sponsors of the German-American Youth Club invited us kids again. To my relief, there were no more Alpine Olympics. Instead, we were to sing carols at the USO Club and the American Base Hospital. The person who signed us up asked who among us could play the piano and, of course, my piano finger number two went up with significance. I was given a small booklet, a GI-issue of American Christmas Carols, so I could accompany my fellow German teenagers in a chorus. Scanning through the booklet, I was unhappy that I was not at all familiar with American Carols. I never had heard about a red-nosed Rudolf, Jingle Bells, nor Two Front Teeth. Nevertheless, we managed to present a nice program to our American hosts. They thought we were cute and, as a reward, served hot cocoa – an incredibly rare treat for us because we had not seen chocolate products for years. I did not, however, know what to do with the candy canes we were given. I had never seen one before and wondered why they were shaped that way. This event put me on the base chaplain's list as a piano player.

That is why, after a year had passed and after I had started to attend the Händel Conservatory in Munich, a military Jeep pulled up in front of our cottage one day. A GI rang our doorbell and, upon entering, introduced himself as "Corporal Crook, Chaplain's Aide at the Base Chapel." Since my Oxford-style school-English at the time did not include the vocabulary to define a "crook," his name did not make a dent on my awareness. He went on, "Chaplain Miller sent me to ask whether you could play the organ for the Sunday services at the base. Our organist quit because of health reasons, and we need a replacement." Hmm, play an organ? As a serious student of piano, I had actually never thought of playing an organ. Even though both instruments have keyboards, it is like asking a psychiatrist whether he can give a good haircut. Corporal Crook elaborated, "The base chapel has a Hammond Organ and, in case you are not familiar with the stops, I can check you out." He appeared worried that he might have to return to the chaplain, Major Miller, and report a failed mission. When I continued to hesitate to answer his question, he tried to raise the incentive by adding, "To play the organ every Sunday and for weekly choir rehearsals, we pay 30 DMs per month – and we would send a staff car to pick you up and take you back home."

His words of money, the 30 DMs, suddenly penetrated my reservations. It would pay my commuter ticket to Munich, to the conservatory, for the whole month! After the recent monetary reform in West Germany, the expense of my train pass, in addition to my music scores and tuition, added up to a difficult monthly challenge. I finally answered. "Ah, yes, I play the organ, not very well, though, and I can commit myself only after I first try the instrument." I never felt so reckless. Cpl. Crook offered, "I can take you to the base now, and you can try out the Hammond, and then I'll bring you right back." That is when it sank in. They actually needed an organist for the coming Sunday! "Let me get some music, and then I'll go," I said. From my shelf, I grabbed some Bach preludes, fugues and the Four Part Chorales. That is when I rode in a Jeep for the first time, with Corporal Crook at the wheel.

<hr />

LEARNING THE LITURGY

I confess it was a matter of impudence that I assumed the position of organist at an American base chapel when I had never even had a bible class, attended a church service, let alone knew how to say the Lord's Prayer – in any lan-

guage. Naturally, as a budding pianist, I knew that preludes
were written to open things and, accordingly, my first semester of form analysis had taught me that a postlude closes
them. I was familiar with Gounod's and Bach's Ave Maria,
but I had never heard the word "hymn" before – nor did I
know any. As the service got under way, unfamiliar with the
order of a church service, my eyes followed with panic the
first church bulletin I had ever seen. Talk about a missionary
crash course!

I had my hands full – not just sight-reading in order to
accompany the congregation with their hymnbooks but,
also, my feet feverishly searched for the right pedal to
change the chord just in time. Surrounding me on my
lonely bench was a well-organized choir of about twenty
American military men and their wives who expected me
to do the introit and to accompany them in whatever else
they had rehearsed. Anyway, I was incredulous when, during the service, Chaplain Miller mentioned to the congregation my name and my new position. No question, after
my first Sunday as the new teenage base organist, I was a
wreck.

Evidently, though, everybody was satisfied because, from
there on – in addition to the Sunday service – choir rehearsals became part of my weekly routine. Living at the opposite
end of town from the airbase, my new commitment every
Wednesday evening brought a big military bus to our door
to pick me up and, from there, return to the base housing
at Williamsville, where the bus filled with members of the
choir. That is how, for the first time, I came in personal contact with Americans. American women's appearance especially interested me: their colorful clothes, big costume jewelry, long polished fingernails, stiff hairdos shaped by hair-
spray, pancake make-up, porcelain complexions, blackened,
beady eyelashes – and their easy chatter while chewing
gum. Despite not understanding much about them, I cautiously liked them.

My ID pass as "Base Organist" at Erding US Air Force Base, 1949.

A PESKY CUSTOMER

Joachim – who spoke English fluently and worked as a communications technician at the base – made a number of friends among Americans. After hours, GIs often asked him to fix their radios, or to build for them an entire audio system from scratch. It was not long before Joachim began to set up a small shop in a section of our shed where he kept tools, gauges, and radio tubes. His business grew rapidly, especially after military personnel were authorized to bring their own cars to Germany, which lead to GIs wanting car radios installed or repaired. Often in the evening or on weekends, they would pull up in our yard for Joachim to do the job. Since bartering was the way of payment, his remunerations generally were in the form of cartons of cigarettes. By 1947, Joachim gave up his employment at the base and, on two sturdy posts, erected a 4' by 4' wooden sign in front of our cottage, eventually with the words "RADIO SEMPT" on a white background. Sempt was the name of the small river that ran through Erding. This was the first step in what

1947, beginning of Joachim's business.
With wife, Bertl, later, in partnership with my father,
the owners of Erding's largest radio and appliance
retail business.

was to become a major electronics and appliance retail store, later located in the center of town.

Intermittently, I continued to take piano lessons from a teacher who was also an organist and a respected composer. His name was Ignaz Doll, and his only son was still a prisoner of war in a Siberian forced labor gulag. Herr Doll eventually helped me prepare for my audition at the Händel Conservatory in Munich, which led to me being admitted for the fall semester of 1947. At home, I was responsible for milking the goat every morning before going to school and, again, in the evening. No one else in the family knew how to milk a goat. In addition, I had to feed the rabbits and clean their pens. My girlfriend Helmi raised rabbits too, and we often visited one another to show off our new baby rabbits.

One evening, as we sat at the table to eat dinner, we heard the gravel in the drive under the wheels of a large black American car that had pulled up in front of the cottage. Joachim, looking through the window, let out a gasp of exasperation. "Not again! This is the third time this Ami is back with the same radio. I don't know what else to do!" He got up and went outside. Through the window, I saw him shake hands with a tall American with lots of ribbons on the chest of his Eisenhower jacket. Looking closer, I noticed that the

Ami smoked a large pipe, the kind with a curved stem made of amber; the carved bowl resembled the head of a maharaja. I recognized it as an outlandish meerschaum pipe. Gesticulating, the Ami urged Joachim to look inside the car, at the dashboard. After some more talk, they both got into the car and drove off. Evidently, the Ami wanted Joachim to hear the static on the radio himself, while the car was moving.

Later, while my mother cleared the table, I took an enamel pot and went into the shed to milk the goat. I first put fresh hay into her crib so she would eat and hold still and, then, swish-swish – just as in the days in Poland when I played Robinson Crusoe with Frederika my goat – I filled the enamel pot.

Left: Wearing one of the blouses my mother made for me of parachute nylon to "barter." Center: Ernst, Architectural student at the University in Munich. Right: Joachim, Technician and budding businessman. All photos approximately 1948

TAKING NOTE OF THE "AMI"

Between my busy days of commuting to Munich to attend the conservatory, dress rehearsals at the opera, practicing piano, taking care of the goat and the rabbits, my job as the base organist, and the choir rehearsals on Wednesdays – I was busy beyond imagination. Occasionally, I still had time to visit with my girlfriends, Helmi and Edith.

Joachim's radio shop flourished, and the majority of his customers were Americans. His previous boss at the base dropped in occasionally to bring him work and radio parts.

Coming home from my Munich train-commute one afternoon, I noticed the Ami with the Meerschaum pipe was leaning against his black Pontiac, parked outside Joachim's radio shop. He looked shy when he said "Hi," as I passed by. I had never heard that word before. "Hi," I responded, as I walked into the house.

1948, Zachary Taylor Everett, stationed in Erding, Germany

THE TRAIN

To attend theory classes, piano instructions, music history and opera workshops at the Händel Conservatory in Munich, I commuted daily by train. As a rule, I left the house at six o'clock every morning to make my way to the train stop, which was recognizable only by a small sign on a pole that announced the name of the suburb as "Altenerding." There was no shelter, not even a bench. For two years, the commuter train was to become my vehicle to a number of memorable postwar experiences.

On winter mornings, when it was still dark and snowing, I had to bundle up and wear heavy boots to wade through deep snow. I usually stood waiting for a while before the small coal-fueled steam engine approached, its single light created a beam of driving snowflakes in its path. The train came to a hissing stop as its squealing breaks cut through the silence of the cold morning. The windows of each car glowed in a dim, yellow light. They were steamed with condensation, indicating the train was crowded with sleepy commuters. I usually rode the first car behind the lo- comotive and struggled through the deep snow to reach the stairs leading to the small platform. Pushing the door open, smelly warm air rushed into my face, smelly people wearing smelly wool clothes sat on slatted oak benches. Yet I was glad the train was heated, remembering that on a recent morning I sat in a car where the heating pipes were cold, and I nearly froze by the time the train reached the "Ostbahnhof," the East Station in Munich.

As I searched for an empty seat, I recognized Fritz, one of the frequent commuters who had become an acquaintance during my daily rides. Waving a rolled up paper above his head to get my attention, he pointed at the empty seat across from his own. After I stowed my tote bag on the luggage rack, I sat down. He smiled at the snow on my boots and commented on the bad weather. Fritz was in his early thirties and athletic in appearance. He often wore an expensive leather trench coat, noticeably the rare product of a black- market deal. Each morning, by the time I boarded the train at the stop in Altenerding, Fritz had already traveled for an hour from Rosenheim, and he continued his ride to Regens- burg for an additional hour after I got off in Munich. Return- ing in the evenings, we often again shared the same train.

Following several months of commuting, our daily con- versations led to a casual friendship. He knew the reason I rode this old train but found it bewildering that I would study music, considering the conditions in Germany, when food and everything else were either scarce or unusual. In turn, I learned that during the war, Fritz had been an aeronautical engineer who used to design airplanes at the Messerschmitt plant in Regensburg. He explained that, after 1945 and the cessation of production of Messerschmitt fighters, he had to return to his home in Rosenheim where he managed his parents' grocery store. Under military occupation, Germans were no longer permitted to build airplanes. As a result, he was not only out of work, but the assumption was he would never again practice his profession. However, after a while, his restlessness led him to convert his aeronautical expertise from building airplanes to designing automobiles. This change was the reason he commuted to Regensburg every day.

Just as I occasionally took a book from my bag to review music history or analyze a Bach fugue, Fritz also used his hours on the train to take folders from his briefcase to scan technical drawings and jot numbers on pages of graph paper. Now and then he turned to me to explain sketches of unusual looking vehicles. I was intrigued by his idea of replacing steering wheels with handlebars, or relying on three wheels instead of four. In fact, I began to dismiss his endeavors as those of typical postwar "spinners," a German term sympathetic of men who, professionally crushed by a lost war and a destroyed economy, ironically visualized a new world of utopian and odd technology. My brothers, each in their field, also pursued futuristic ideas – Ernst, in the form of intricate suspended bridges or the extremes of energy-conserving subterranean architecture; and Joachim, in the technology of electronic robotics.

One morning, after getting on my train, an excited Fritz Fend greeted me with the news that he had completed the prototype of his car. In fact, it was to be the first postwar German micro-car – a single passenger model originally designed for war-injured, the many amputees – a vehicle he called the "Fend Flitzer." Trying to pay closer attention than before, I carefully looked at his drawings which depicted several three-wheeled cars, each with an uncanny resemblance to airplanes – however, without the wings. I found his two-passenger models fascinating. They showed seats that were in a tandem arrangement just as on a fighter plane. Indeed, even the top of the car was a hinged Plexiglas bubble that opened like a cockpit.

It was on this old commuter train in 1948, when a greatly exhilarated Fritz Fend announced to me that his former employer, Willy Messerschmitt, eager to fill his empty airplane factory, had just given permission to proceed to build the three-wheeled micro-cars, whose genesis I had come to witness. The micro-cars were to become the first postwar German-built automobiles. Fritz Fend's peculiar three-wheeled Messerschmitt cars, later also with four wheels, were built until 1964 and grew into a popular sight on German city streets as well as on Alpine roads.

They were to be remembered for many years by Germans of my generation. To this day, Messerschmitt Clubs flourish in Germany and the rest of Europe, as well as in England. Volkswagen recently reviewed Fritz Fend's passenger tandem designs with hinged cockpits in preparation for their 2004 Production…

1948 Fend's tandem Messerschmitt minicar, "FEND FLITZER" and in
2004 the VW with revived Fend's tandem seating

THE TRAIN – AGAIN

I glanced at my watch and took note that, because a class at the conservatory had been cancelled, I was an hour early. Instead of standing around on the ramp waiting for my train to take me back to Erding, I opted to spend the extra hour in the restaurant of the "Ostbahnhof," the East Rail Station in Munich. I always enjoyed the atmosphere of the restaurant. There, at white linen-covered tables, one could find travelers from all over the world – men from the Orient wearing turbans, diplomats in pinstriped suits, women in saris, perhaps a Bavarian housewife with her dachshund, or even a tabloid celebrity in a garish new-look getup. A waiter in a tuxedo and a towel over his arm scurried to take orders.

The year was 1948 and, in Munich, rubble still covered bombed-out city blocks. However, the economy of occupied West Germany had just passed a currency reform which, after the postwar years of famine and barter system, stirred the beginnings of free enterprise. The new currency also left most of us students in a state of painful poverty. Despite being only seventeen and money-poor, sitting in the railroad station's restaurant made me feel sophisticated and grown-up, especially when I ordered the waiter to bring me one cigarette with my coffee. The cigarette was placed carefully on a saucer and cost one D-Mark. Even though I was hungry, my ineptness in economics motivated me to puff this single cigarette in a pretentious moment of prosperity. Besides, what money I had on me was not enough anyway to have bought a bratwurst and a roll.

As I basked in my adolescent maladjustment, I suddenly heard a familiar voice call my name. "Gudrun, what a terrific coincidence!" There was Tony, the image of an athlete and tanned from skiing trips to the Dolomites. He approached my table and grabbed my hand with a hand kiss. "May I join you?" he asked, as he pulled out a chair to sit down. Tony was a family friend and a former fellow engineering student during my brother Ernst's time at the Polytechnic Institute. I knew that Tony worked as a cameraman with "Bavaria Film Studios," one among the pioneer German postwar movie industries. Putting his elbow on the table, he came right to the point as he explained, "We are shooting a film for the next few days and nights here at the station, and we need some extras. Would you like to sign up? The studio pays extras thirty DMs per day or night. Tonight we will film crowd scenes at one of the side ramps, people getting in and out of a train."

I had never heard of such a situation before, but did comprehend that for thirty DMs, I could buy a number of piano books! "You mean I just need to get in and out of a train?" I asked with skepticism. Tony laughed, "Yes, and you may have to do it a number of times. We do re-shoots until we get it just right." "Gee," I said, "but my mother would be worried if I didn't come home." Tony smiled, "Can't you call and ask her permission?" he asked, "And give her my compliments. I am sure she will approve. Tomorrow morning you would just take the first train to go home. We have a commissary near the ramp. They serve a dynamite goulash and there, between scenes, you would also meet our stars, Peter Possetti and Ilse Werner." My mouth dropped open, "You mean they are here at the station?" I asked in disbelief. "Yes, most of the time," Tony answered with a grin. "By the way, the recruiter pays in advance, and you will be given a pass to get into the commissary." That is when I realized I should take Tony up on his offer. Actually, I was very hungry when I thought of the goulash. "I will call my mother," I said, getting up.

1947, as Piano Major at the Haendel Conservatory in Munich

Typical coal train, similar to what I commuted on to Munich, 1946-50.

DRIVING LEO'S BUS

For Sunday services at the Erding Air Base, Corporal Crook, in a staff car from the motor pool, usually picked me up at my house. After church, I was taken back home in the same manner. There were a few occasions when the motor pool was delayed, and Chaplain Miller drove me home in his Mercury. I admired him greatly.

I began to enjoy my job as the base organist. As time passed, I added new church music to my organ repertoire, and I actually looked forward to Wednesday evening's choir rehearsals. Following the rehearsal one evening, and after dropping off the choir members the American base housing at Williamsville, I asked Leo, the German driver, to let me drive the bus. He looked surprised that I would be interested in such an absurdity, but then he pulled over and made room in front of the steering wheel. "Wait, don't go away, Leo!" I exclaimed, "You'll have to shift for me! I don't know how." Therefore, Leo sat down on the front seat, and off we went. Obligingly, he shifted the big gear handle for me each time I pushed down the clutch at intersections or stop signs. What fun to drive a big bus! It was getting dark, and I was glad nobody could see me rumble through town driving a big Army bus. I found that when I accelerated the engine between Leo's shifting and my pushing down the clutch, the bus did not lurch as much. "Donnerwetter," Leo said, "Sie geben Zwischengas wie ein Lastwagen-fahrer!" (Something like: "Wow! You are revving the engine between shifts, just like a savvy truck driver!") Evidently, that was a good thing to do, and I was very proud of myself. I know now that driving a bus without a license was my clos-est brush with the law, without being a juvenile delinquent.

The following Sunday, after service, I was waiting for Corporal Crook and his jeep to take me home again, but he was delayed. As I stood there, Joachim's Ami, the one with the chronic car radio, stepped through the door with Chap-lain Miller. When I commented I was still waiting for my ride, the Ami offered, "May I take you home? I know where you live."

\~\~\~\~\~\~\~\~\~\~\~\~\~\~\~\~\~\~

THE HUNTER

A few weeks later, I think on a Saturday afternoon, the Ami and his Meerschaum pipe showed up with a dead deer in the trunk of his Pontiac. American occupation troops, who were interested in hunting in Germany, were allowed to do so only if accompanied by a German "Jaeger," a professional forester. I suppose this regulation was to protect wildlife from being killed out of season, or in too many numbers. Knowing how scarce food was for Germans, the Ami thought of us. Besides, what could he have done with a deer carcass in his barracks? I recall that the head of the deer was shot off, therefore I couldn't tell whether it ever had antlers. After my father skinned and gutted the animal, my mother was delighted to prepare the venison. It had been some time since we enjoyed roasted deer.

That is when I found out the Ami's name was Zachary. In Bavaria, such a name might be changed into "Zacherl," an endearing nickname for the German "Zacharias." The next day, being Sunday, and after church service, Zacherl stood at the door of the chapel, this time waiting to take me home. When we arrived in front of our cottage, I invited him to join us at dinner, to share his deer my mother had prepared with Spaetzle. He did eat the roast deer – without a second helping, though. I had the impression that Zacherl disliked venison very much.

THE "GIFT"*

Normally, my commuter train returned to Erding late in the afternoon. Occasionally, however, as part of my studies at the conservatory, I attended opera at the Prinzregenten Theater with my student pass. That is when I used the eleven o'clock Theater Train, which brought me home at midnight. On one of those late nights, when my family was already asleep, I silently opened the door so not to wake anyone. As I reached for the light switch inside the door, I heard Murrax running excitedly to greet me. I noticed something was wrong with him, because he went into some kind of seizure. He began to choke and cough, his mouth wide open and his tongue turned blue. I quickly put my books down and cradled him in my lap. Stroking his head, I tried to calm him down. In fact, I had just recently begun to notice these episodes – they were always triggered by something that excited him, like the arrival of the mailman, or even the sound of another dog barking in the distance. He became short of breath, choked and gasped for air. Lately, these spells had begun to occur more frequently and lasted longer. Each time I felt helpless because there was nothing I could do.

Next morning, following this latest episode, my mother called the veterinarian. Later that day, after I had just gotten home from Munich on my afternoon train, Dr. Schneider arrived. Again, Murrax became terribly excited and gave the doctor a firsthand demonstration of one of his seizures. Dr. Schneider lifted him on the couch and firmly massaged his back. Then, with concern in his voice, he asked me, "Is Murrax your dog, Fraulein Koppe?" "Yes" I said, "I grew up with him. I got him when I was just five and he was my best pal through my entire childhood." I continued to explain how Murrax moved with us from Freilassing to Poland in 1939; and how, at the end of the war, he escaped the Soviets with us; and when he survived the blizzard and weeks of trek on a horse wagon; and how he later walked miles with us, even on the Autobahn, to finally reach the West. "He experienced many dreadful moments and the famine, and..." As I recounted Murrax's life I started to sob.

Trying to comfort me, Dr. Schneider said, "It looks like Murrax was an important part of your life and he had a loving owner, but he also had a pretty rough time for a while. We all did," he added wistfully. "I am sorry, but I can not do much for Murrax, Fraulein." He continued: "It is still difficult to obtain veterinary medicines, especially to treat heart failure. In fact, some are based on caffeine. For this reason, try to sweeten a small cup of strong coffee and entice Murrax to drink a teaspoonful a few times a day to stimulate his heart. Of course, caffeine won't cure his condition." His frustration was audible when Dr. Schneider explained: "I regret to recommend that we put Murrax to sleep to ease his suffering, but I don't even have morphine." I started to sob again. Dr. Schneider then rose and, preparing to leave, he said, "With other words, I can't put him down." Seeing my tears, he tried to divert my pain when he added with a laconic twist, "My mother-in-law would know a way..." And he quietly closed the door behind him.

I heard the car door slam outside and, for a few moments, I sat wiping my eyes, with Murrax on my lap. Suddenly, Dr. Schneider appeared in the door again. He handed me a vial with large white pills. "Here" he said, "I found some Luminal in my bag. Crush the pills between two teaspoons and dissolve them with water by shaking them vigorously in a small bottle." Continuing to instruct me how to administer the solution, he inserted his index finger into the side of Murrax's mouth and pulled his cheek away from the teeth to demonstrate how the opening of a small bottle could easily be inserted into the hollow space. "Then lift Murrax's head straight up while you empty the liquid deep into the side of his mouth. You will find him asleep next morning – he won't wake again." He paused for a moment and said, "Put the vial on a shelf and, if his seizures get worse, you will know when to give him the pills." Taking both my hands, he added, "I know you can do it."

Dr. Schneider stopped at the door once more and, turning to my mother, he said, "The pills will not be on the bill. They are my gift." With that, he left.

It is a strange coincidence that the word "Gift" in German means poison...

*MURRAX and I. **Left:** 1936 Freilassing **Center:** 1943 in Dolsk, Poland*
***Right:** 1948, in Erding, Germany*

"DER SCHMUSER"
AN EPILOG BY MURRAX

Mmmm, my head fits perfectly under her chin. There... Whenever I sit on her lap like this, and push my head under her chin, she is very pleased and calls me "Schmoozer" and all kinds of sweet names. Then she scratches the place behind my ears. Other times she can be so cruel, though, like when I have to wait for the family to finish dinner first, before I am being fed. It smells so good while they eat. Fortunately, I'm the type of dog that doesn't drool. Some breeds' lips hang loose like wet flannel; they are hound dogs and slobber all over themselves when they smell food. Whereas I, being a classy terrier, am proud that my lips are tight, and I don't drool.

Finally, I hear her scrape the leftovers from everybody's plate into hers so she can put it under her chair, where I normally eat my dinner. I barely start, when her kid, the six-year-old, gets up and leans down to razz me by pretending to take my plate right out from under my hungry snout, just so she can hear me growl and see me flash my teeth. She is a real belligerent brat. The other day, when she did that, I nipped her finger very hard and, after it swelled into a big welt, she gave me a "watschen." That's a Bavarian slap across the back of my neck. But then, to make up with me, she gives me a caramel – and when it gets stuck in my molars, and when I have to chew and chew and chew, she goes into screaming ninnies. She can't get enough of my dilemma. And, before I finish the caramel, she already gives me another one – and again she goes crazy laughing, while she watches me chew like I never chewed before. The caramels do taste good, though. And then she has another fling with my dignity: she puts me into her doll carriage and pushes me around. I hate it when she puts that dumb bonnet on my head and lays me on my back on the pink lace pillow. No self-respecting wire terrier likes to lie on his back inside a wobbly doll buggy, especially when she races across the street to her girl-friend's house and pushes the carriage off the sidewalk with a big bump. That's when I jump out. I've had it! It takes me a moment to scrape the bonnet off my head with my paw, and then I leave the scene. She now has a fit. Wanting me back in her doll buggy, she yells, "Murrax! Murrax!" But her voice grows faint as I sprint down the street.

I am on my way to that cute dachshund I met the other day near the bench in front of the town's fountain. Oh my, what's that overpowering odor? I have to stop and check! Boy-oh-boy, a dead pigeon by the side of the road! Finding this cadaver is such perfect timing! I immediately throw myself on top of it and, rolling on my back, I feel the mushy stuff beginning to stick to the fur around my shoul-ders. I can just see the Dachsy go wild when she gets a whiff of me! Against my expectations, this courtship takes exceptionally long. After two days of hanging around her house, my stench is almost worn off, and I am extremely hungry.

I finally catch the Dachsy and have my way with her. And, just as I am ready to leave, the front door opens and the Dachsy is called into the house. That's when I hear a big bang and, at the same moment the man in the door is envel-oped in a puff of smoke, I feel an incredible, searing pain at the rear of my rump. That son of a gun hit me with buck-shot! I run home as fast as I can.

It's been two days since I had jumped out of the kid's doll carriage, and now the whole family is so glad to see me back. There is much yelling and hand-wringing about my condition, when they discover and probe with their fingers the pellets under my skin. I am then given a bath with lots of soap to get rid of the stinky cadaver crap in my fur, and the crusty blood from the buckshot turns the bathwater into a bright pink. After I am clean and toweled into my fluffy, cutest self, I jump on her lap and tightly fit my head under her chin, and she calls me "Schmuser" and again scratches my ears. Later, the brat stuffs me back into her doll carriage – and takes me on another bumpy ride…"

~~~~~~~~~~~~~~~~~~~~~~~~~~~~~

A SUMMER OF MUSIC AND ROMANCE

In 1949, instead of a summer break, I decided to take two courses at the conservatory for needed credits. One was in piano performance, conducted by Geza Anda, a name that years later would gain international fame among the world's greatest pianists, and the other was an opera workshop, directed by a woman who happened to bear the same last name as mine, Frau Professor Dr. Koppe. The courses gave me the opportunity to study with two great artists, as well as regularly attend the "Prinzregenten Theater," the only one of three Munich operas that had been restored from bombing-damage. Most of my attendances were for dress rehearsals, which ended late in the afternoons.

During this busy summer schedule, Sunday mornings continued to be taken up by my job as base organist. There, since the previous fall, it had become almost routine that after the service, Zach, the Ami with the Meerschaum pipe, waited to take me home in his black Pontiac. And one afternoon he asked my mother whether he could take me to an American movie at the base theater. To my surprise, my mother seemed very pleased and wished us a good time. And that's how I began to date Zach.

Zach took great pleasure in visiting our family. Many evenings he played chess with my father, and both my brothers had developed a comfortable friendship with him, Joachim, having first met him as a customer during the previous spring, and Ernst, working as architect at the base, had met him there at the engineering office.

Gradually we learned about Zach's personal background. He showed us pictures of his family in the Midwest and mentioned that he no longer had parents, and that he was the youngest of five brothers. He spoke about his military career, and in the course of conversations, I learned that he had been awarded a direct officers commission upon his return from Siapan where, between 1944 and 1945, he had flown 36 missions on a B29 over Japan, missions of which one third were lost in combat; and finally I learned that among the many ribbons on his uniform was the Distinguished Flying Cross. The more I found out about Zach, the more I sensed his quiet strength and confidence.

As the summer progressed, Munich became our frequent meeting place where, after my classes at the Conservatory, Zach would wait for me in his parked car at the foot of the tall column that held the nearby monument of the "Angel of Peace," its golden wings spread wide against the blue Bavarian sky. It is to this day one of the most famous Munich landmarks located in Bogenhausen, the residential section of Munich, where immediately after the war, villas had been confiscated to accommodate DPs and their Black Market operations. By now, the rightful owners had returned to their homes; and in general, Munich was beginning to show progress of reconstruction, with most of the rubble removed.

Occasionally on Saturday evenings after dinner at the club, Zach escorted me to the opera. And I shall never forget – nor forgive – when during the second act of La Boheme, I gently had to jab his shoulder because he had fallen asleep. On the way home, he offered a reasonable explanation: he had been up since five that morning to go deer hunting, and all that hiking through the woods for hours with so much fresh the air, and so forth... Actually that evening I took note that this American was not fond of opera.

Then one day on the way to Garmisch, Zach stopped the car and asked me to get behind the wheel because he had decided I should learn to drive. In this endeavor, I still shudder when I recall his reckless trust in me. Sitting in the passenger's seat, he calmly smoked his Meerschaum pipe with me tooling along on the Autobahn doing a hundred km an hour. However, he did become visibly perturbed, when I later tried to park in front of the American Club, but did not know how to shift down fast enough, while in a seemingly deliberate and flirtatious manner the bumper of the bucking car kept nudging the back of the knees of a hapless young corporal, who was trying to get out of my way. That's when Zach took the pipe from his mouth for a moment.

In September Zach turned 25, and we surprised him by celebrating his birthday with a special mocha torte that my mother had brought from her favorite "Konditorei," the pastry shop next to Erding's old tower. I never saw anyone as touched as Zach was. He later confided in me that this had been his first birthday cake.

wwwwwwwwwwwwwwwww

I MARRIED THE AMERICAN,
ZACHARY EVERETT

In the Fall of 1949, I completed my second year at the Händel Conservatory with a certificate in Piano Performance. Zach's assignment in Germany was coming to an end, which meant that in April of 1950 he would have to return to the United States. Zach had asked me to marry him and given me a diamond engagement ring.

In comparison to the present ease of international travel, a journey between two continents in 1949 was complicated – and rare. Zach and I knew that once he departed, immigration laws and other circumstances could keep us separated for an undeterminable time. I found the possibility that I might never see him again unbearable. For this reason, I needed to make the decision to marry him – and leave Germany with him.

The legal preparations for me to immigrate proved to be enormously elaborate and created a colossal folder of paperwork. In order to receive a permit from military authorities to marry a German citizen, Zach too, was overwhelmed with red tape. He was even requested to provide three written character references of myself, furnished by friends of his who had met me, perhaps only once. The most caring and encouraging person in the efforts to overcome our obstacles was Chaplain Miller. He had become our friend.

Zach and I were married January 24, 1950, and left Germany the following April.

Our Wedding in Erding, Germany, January 24, 1950.

L-R: *my father, Adolf Koppe, Ernst, Joachim.* ***Front:*** *my mother and the New Everetts*

VI.
Reflections

2005

ARE THEY STILL THERE?

In the early 1980s, living in New England, thousands of miles from Poland, I held in my hand a letter from Dolsk, written in Polish by a young woman I had never met. It was the time of the Cold War, and through a friend's effort I had found the family, actually the offspring, of one of our former employees in Dolsk, with whom I intended to take up correspondence. Knowing that Poles still suffered similar shortages in daily necessities that I remember having suffered in Post War Germany, I began to send them several packages with food, coffee, clothing and other things that I knew they could not buy. In return I received letters of profuse gratitude and enclosed pictures of a young couple and their little girl with a taffeta bow in her hair, and of a nine-year old boy next to his pet mongrel dog.

Since I can not speak Polish, except for a few terrible words I had picked up at the stables when I was a horse-crazy little girl in Dolsk, I had to write my letters to the Polish couple in German which, unfortunately, they were unable to read. I did eventually find out that the young woman's name was Hedwig, and to my relief soon, after a few hapless exchanges, a type-written page of translation into German began to accompany her letters, each responding in precise detail to my previous letter. In one of Hedwig's subsequent letters I found almost obscured by the wording of the translation that a retired priest was the anonymous interpreter of our correspondence. He was to become the third persona in this arrangement. Obviously, as the interpreter of our correspondence he knew everything I was writing to Hedwig and vice versa, but Hedwig was the one who would not know if I enclosed in my letter anything intended for the interpreter.

After several months of our communications, and to my utter amazement one day I found enclosed in Hedwig's letter a picture of myself as a little girl standing under the door of the house in Poland, and another of myself sitting in my pony cart. Both photos were the same as the ones in our family album. This implied that somebody had found a box of loose, extra photos that may have been left behind when we fled from Poland in 1945. More over, among these personal pictures of myself as a child, were several of the house, obviously taken forty years later, during the time the letter was written, showing its awful deterioration. Conspicuously, the pictures illustrated the house from the identical angle as the ones taken before we left Poland in 1945. This suggested that the photographer of the more recent images had access to the old pictures that had been left behind. Recognizable by the similar perspective of the shots, the photographer's obvious intention was to invite comparisons.

The day I received the pictures in Hedwig's letter I discovered something new at the end of the type-written, accompanying translation. It was signed with a cautious, tiny pencil-written name, "Johann."

With this deliberate hint of identification I suddenly felt compelled to confide in Johann, the priest, my recollection of the hidden paintings in the sealed flue on the second floor of the house in 1945, and to ask him if he could please check whether they were still there, so that they can be secured or whatever needs to be done with them. In short, knowing that Hedwig could not read my German, in my next letter to her and discreetly, with as few words as possible, I communicated with Johann, the translator, to inform him about the hidden paintings.

An unusually long time passed. In the meantime I had sent another package with food and clothing to Hedwig, before I again received a letter from Poland. This time, instead of the type-written page, the translation was in form of a hand-written note which was difficult to read. Among the usual comments of joy upon re-

ceiving the package, Hedwig' letter explained how sad
she was that the old priest had suddenly passed away,
but that one of her neighbors, who was proficient in
German, was willing to carry on future translations of
our correspondence...

*1945, the main building and kitchen wing while we lived in the house,
before we fled from Poland*

*1981 the house from similar angles as above, enclosed by the Polish
priest in the last letter.*

A TRAIL OF BETRAYAL

Dietrich Bonhoeffer, not a politician, but a German Lutheran pastor and theologian, was an exemplar of sac-
rificial faith: he opposed the Nazis from the beginning, was
eventually imprisoned in Buchenwald and hung by the Ge-
stapo in 1945. *The Cost of Discipleship*, first published in
German in 1937, was Bonhoeffer's answer to the questions,

"What did Jesus mean to say to us? What is his will for us today?"

He and another Lutheran clergyman, Dr. Hans Schoenfeld and several Jesuits, joined in the support of "Die Abwehr," a group which included Count Helmut von Moltke, Col. Canaris, and a number of German generals. Die Abwehr, a resistance movement, was committed to overthrow Hitler's government, possibly by assassination. The history of Dr. Bonhoeffer in connection with the German underground resistance against the Nazis, is a case of betrayal. It was doomed the moment Banhoeffer contacted the Allies for assistance.

In view of the indecent peace treaty of Versailles following WWI, Bonhoeffer's concern was to make contact with the Allies in hopes of securing assistance and to obtain assurances that the kind of peace the Allies would be willing to make with Germany would be acceptable, if Hitler's government were overthrown.

With this mission in mind, Prof. Dr. Bonhoeffer and Dr. Hans Schoenfeld, a member of the Foreign Relations Bureau of the German Evangelical Church, traveled to Stockholm in May of 1942 under forged papers in order to meet with Bishop Bell, the Anglican bishop of Chichester, England. The German pastors informed the bishop of the plans of the underground conspirators, with the hopes that the Western Allies would assist if needed, and that they would be willing to make a decent peace with a post-Nazi Germany. The pastors asked for an answer by either a private message or a public announcement. To convince the Anglican bishop that the anti-Hitler conspiracy was serious, and to add credence to their mission, Bonhoeffer provided the bishop with a list of names of the underground leaders – both military and others. The list was the most authoritative and up-to-date information the Allies had on plans by the German underground resistance.

Eventually this disclosure, however, cost them their lives. Bishop Bell turned the message over to Anthony Eden, the British foreign secretary, but no response resulted. More underground contacts were made by other conspirators with the Allies in Switzerland through Allen Dulles, who headed the OSS until the end of the war, also to no avail.

The Allies' indifference finally lead Dr. Schoenfeld to warn Dulles that if the Western democracies refuse to consider a decent peace with an anti-Nazi German regime, the conspirators would turn to the Soviets for assistance – but Dulles still did not respond. Stalin, however offered to initiate talks for a separate peace from the Western Allies. In fact Ribbentrop in his defense at the Nuremberg Trial, placed great emphasis on his own efforts to negotiate peace with the Russians. Secret German papers are still to be opened to reveal this chapter of history – or it may continue to be too "inconvenient" for those who hold the copyrights to post-WWII politicized history.

Tragically, the Western Allies never explored the option of assisting the German underground. Instead, after a ceaseless six-year effort to destroy Hitler and the Nazi regime, the German conspirators were ultimately defeated because, three months after Bonhoeffer had made contact with the British, Canaris, Oster, Dohnanyi, Bonhoeffer and a number of other conspirators, were arrested on July 20, 1944.

In April 1945, barely three weeks before V-E day, the SS stripped them naked and led them out of their cells where they deliberately hanged them in a manner that took them half an hour to die. All in all, the Allies' rejection of Bonhoeffer's plea resulted in the execution and torture of more than 157 German officers. Among them 15 Lieutenant Colonels, 17 Colonels, 13 Generals, one field marshal, and 9 Counts. Another 5,000 Germans were to follow them to the gallows – days before Germany's defeat.

END RESULT?

Between July 20, 1944 and May 8, 1945, ten million people were killed in the European theater of World War II, more than in the preceding five years of the most devastating conflict in human history.

After 1945, President Roosevelt issued a directive that there was to be no printed mention of the German Resistance having ever existed. This ban remained in effect well after the war throughout occupied Germany. Thus history suggests, that the Allies were not interested in peace, nor the overthrow of Hitler – but in the Unconditional Surrender, contingent on the total destruction of Germany.

~~~~~~~~~~~~~~~~~~~~~~~~~~~

CYNICISM OF COMMEMORATION

April 1995 was the 50th anniversary of Bonhoeffer's execution. Many American Newspapers' religious sections made much ado about his heroic legacy. And there were commemorative services in numerous Protestant churches throughout America. Bonhoeffer's biographer and his niece came to Washington to attend services – one at the National Holocaust Museum and an other at the National Cathedral. They were cynical "honors" for a martyr.

Dresden and burning of corpses

Left: *Wurzburg*   ***Right***: *Duesseldorf*

Nuremberg

Left: *Kassel*   ***Right***: *Frankfurt*

Hamburg: Firestorm over the city

Hamburg

Berlin and Soviet tanks at the Berlin Reichstag

OTHER LOSSES, by James Baque: Mass Deaths of German Prisoners at the Hands of the French and Americans, after World War Two. The book describes the fate German soldiers who had surrendered to General Eisenhower's forces at the end of WWII. Due to lack of shelter, starvation and exposure, millions of them died. As Mr. Bacque points out, instead of POWs, an entire new category of "Disarmed Enemy Forces," DEF, was created. Its only purpose was to avoid having to feed and house these millions of ex-soldiers, and thereby bypass the Geneva convention, to which America was a signatory.

HUMAN SUFFERING IN GERMANY 1945

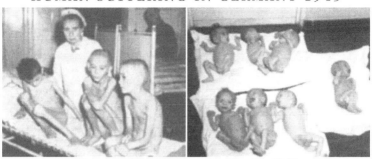

German children - victims of famine 1945

Homeless in bombed out City

ETHNIC CLEANSING: Trek - 15 million ethnic Germans were expelled from East Europe, in the process two million perished through violence, torture, starvation and exposure to the Winter of 1944-45

13824010R00121

Made in the USA
San Bernardino, CA
08 August 2014